Pakistan

Pakistan

BY ANN HEINRICHS

Enchantment of the World
Second Series

Children's Press®

A Division of Scholastic Inc.

NEW YORK   TORONTO   LONDON   AUCKLAND   SYDNEY
MEXICO CITY   NEW DELHI   HONG KONG
DANBURY, CONNECTICUT

Frontispiece: Village women with earthenware pots

Consultant: Dr. Amy J. Johnson, Department of History, Berry College, Mount Berry, GA

Please note: All statistics are as up-to-date as possible at the time of publication.

Book production by Herman Adler Design

Library of Congress Cataloging-in-Publication Data

Heinrichs, Ann.
  Pakistan / by Ann Heinrichs.
      p. cm.—(Enchantment of the world. Second series)
  ISBN 0-516-24248-2
1. Pakistan—Juvenile literature. [1. Pakistan.] I. Title. II. Series.
DS376.9.H45 2004
954.91—dc21   2002156712

CHILDREN'S PRESS and associated logos are trademarks and or registered
trademarks of Scholastic Library Publishing. SCHOLASTIC and associated logos
are trademarks and or registered trademarks of Scholastic Inc.
  2 3 4 5 6 7 8 9 10 R 13 12 11 10 09 08 07 06

Pakistan

Contents

CHAPTER

 ONE   A Land of Tradition 8

TWO   Mountains, Valleys, Deserts, and Plains 14

 THREE   Animal and Plant Communities 28

FOUR   Ancient Kingdoms and a Modern Nation 38

FIVE   The Struggle for Democracy 52

 **SIX**   Pakistanis at Work 62

SEVEN   People of Many Cultures 76

EIGHT   Spiritual Life 84

NINE   Arts, Culture, and Sports 98

TEN   Everyday Life 116

A fertile valley

Timeline................... **128**

Fast Facts................. **130**

To Find Out More.......... **134**

Index..................... **136**

Pakistani children

A Land of Tradition

Yasmin is a twelve-year-old girl in a small Pakistani village. Her family is neither rich nor poor, but somewhere in between. They are farmers who live in a small, clay-brick house.

Every day Yasmin gets up at 6:00 A.M. She dresses as most Pakistanis do—in a long, loose-fitting shirt and trousers—and puts on her long headscarf. She says her prayers and eats a breakfast of eggs, bread, and tea. Then she walks to school. Yasmin's older sister, who is fifteen, has already finished primary school. Now she stays at home helping her mother with household chores.

At school Yasmin takes classes in science, math, social studies, religious studies, English, and Urdu, Pakistan's official language. She loves school and is first in her class. Her dream is to become a doctor. During recess she plays hopscotch with her classmates. Boys and girls in Pakistan attend separate schools, so all her playmates are girls. Yasmin knows she is lucky. Most girls in her village do not attend school at all.

Opposite: **A Pakistani girl does her homework in a field.**

A teacher leads a class of girls in a local school.

When she gets home, she does her homework. Then she feeds the cattle and chickens, washes dishes, cleans the courtyard, and makes tea. She has some time to play with her friends before prayers and dinner. Yasmin's village has electricity, so she watches a little television before bedtime at 9:00 P.M.

Yasmin is better off than many other girls her age. Her family is financially stable and welcome the chance to send her to school. The vast majority of Pakistanis are very poor. They labor in the arid fields or spend long hours in factories and mills. The most traditional Pakistanis see no value in educating girls. Traditions are strong, but some of the old ways are changing. If Yasmin is lucky, she may realize her dream of becoming a doctor.

Yasmin's daily life reflects her society in many ways. Like most other Pakistanis, she is a devout Muslim—a follower of the religion of Islam. For Muslims, religion gives meaning to many facets of life. Islam has inspired much of Pakistani art and literature. For many families, Islam is the guiding force in their values and everyday lives. Mosques, Muslim houses of worship, rise over even the smallest villages. Several times a day devout Muslims stop their work to kneel in prayer. Generosity, hospitality, modest clothing, and strict moral values are all signs of Pakistanis' deep-seated faith.

Pakistan is a young nation built upon ancient kingdoms. Only in 1947 did Pakistan become an independent country. However, human societies have flourished there for five thousand years. The region that is now Pakistan was home to the Indus Valley Civilization, one of the oldest cultures in the

Pakistani Muslims offer prayers outside a mosque in Karachi.

world. Its people built elegant homes and fabulous monuments. Later, under the Mughal Empire, people created beautiful poetry and music and built magnificent mosques. For Pakistanis, this rich cultural heritage remains a source of pride and inspiration.

A fertile valley flourishes alongside an arid landscape in Pakistan.

Geographically, Pakistan is a land of extremes. It has snow-capped peaks, deep valleys, fertile plains, and arid deserts. Some of the world's highest mountains tower over northern Pakistan. In the south, sandy beaches line the Arabian Sea coast. Flowing from north to south is the Indus River, whose waters bring life to the farms of the central plains.

Located on the South Asian subcontinent, Pakistan lies in one of the world's political "hot spots." Its neighbors are Iran, Afghanistan, China, and India. These countries have seen some of the most serious conflicts of modern times. Pakistan has often found itself in the center of these clashes.

At home, Pakistan has had its share of problems, too. Since its birth as a nation, Pakistan has shifted back and forth between democratic governments and military regimes. Conflicts continue today as the country struggles against terrorist activities.

For Yasmin and other young Pakistanis, this turmoil is a worrisome daily reality. Yet their cultural traditions bring them joy, honor, and pride. They hope to carry these traditions forward into a peaceful future.

Opposite: **Geopolitical map of Pakistan**

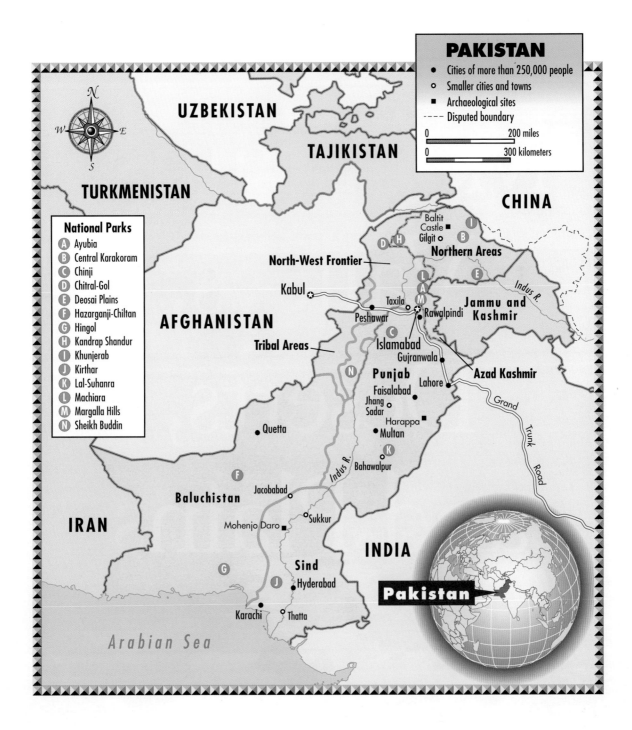

PAKISTAN

- ● Cities of more than 250,000 people
- ○ Smaller cities and towns
- ■ Archaeological sites
- --- Disputed boundary

0   200 miles
0   300 kilometers

National Parks
- Ⓐ Ayubia
- Ⓑ Central Karakoram
- Ⓒ Chinji
- Ⓓ Chitral-Gol
- Ⓔ Deosai Plains
- Ⓕ Hazarganji-Chiltan
- Ⓖ Hingol
- Ⓗ Kandrap Shandur
- Ⓘ Khunjerab
- Ⓙ Kirthar
- Ⓚ Lal-Suhanra
- Ⓛ Machiara
- Ⓜ Margalla Hills
- Ⓝ Sheikh Buddin

UZBEKISTAN

TAJIKISTAN

TURKMENISTAN

CHINA

Baltit Castle ■
Gilgit ○
Northern Areas

North-West Frontier

Kabul ☆

Taxila ●
Peshawar ●
Rawalpindi ☆
Jammu and Kashmir

Indus R.

AFGHANISTAN

Tribal Areas

Islamabad
Gujranwala ●
Punjab
Azad Kashmir
Faisalabad
Jhang Sadar ○
Harappa ■
Multan ●
Lahore ●

Grand Trunk Road

Quetta ●

Baluchistan

Indus R.

Jacobabad ○

Bahawalpur ●

Mohenjo Daro ■
Sukkur ○

INDIA

IRAN

Sind
Hyderabad ●
Thatta ○
Karachi ●

Pakistan

Arabian Sea

Mountains, Valleys, Deserts, and Plains

P AKISTAN IS A LAND OF LUSH VALLEYS, BARREN DESERTS, and jagged mountain peaks. Many ancient traders and their camel caravans once passed through this land, carrying goods between Asia and Europe. For centuries, the main trade route through Pakistan was the Silk Route. Traders on this fabled route carried silk, spices, and other precious goods from China through central Asia to Arabia. Invaders from all sides swept into Pakistan, too. Both traders and invaders brought new peoples and cultures into the area.

Pakistan is located in south Asia. It's part of a region called the Indian subcontinent. India lies to the east of Pakistan, and China borders the northeast. To the north and west is Afghanistan, and Iran is on the southwest. Southern Pakistan touches the Arabian Sea, a part of the Indian Ocean. Coursing down the country from north to south is the Indus River. One of the world's earliest civilizations flourished in the Indus River Valley.

The Kashmir region in the northeast is a disputed area. When India and Pakistan were divided in 1947, both countries claimed Kashmir. They fought over the region many times. In 1972 the two countries agreed to a boundary, or "line of control," through Kashmir. Now Pakistan governs northern and western Kashmir. Southern and southwestern Kashmir became the Indian state of Jammu and Kashmir. Ladakh, the easternmost part of Kashmir, is partly under Chinese control.

Opposite: **Mountain streams in Pakistan are fed by glaciers and melting snow.**

Kashmir region of Pakistan

Pakistan's portion of Kashmir consists of two areas. One is Azad Kashmir (*Azad* means "free"). The other is the Gilgit and Baltistan regions of the Northern Areas. The Northern Areas is a huge mountainous territory bordering China.

The Northern Mountains

High mountains cover northern Pakistan. Among these snow-capped peaks are some of the highest and most rugged mountains on earth. Ten of the world's thirty highest peaks are in regions controlled wholly or partly by Pakistan. Massive

Pakistan's Geographical Features

Borders: Iran to the southwest, Afghanistan to the west and north, China to the northeast, India to the east, and the Arabian Sea (part of the Indian Ocean) to the south

Area: 310,402 square miles (803,937 sq km)

Highest Elevation: K2 (Mount Godwin-Austen) in Kashmir, 28,251 feet (8,611 m) above sea level

Lowest Elevation: Sea level along the coast

Average Annual Precipitation: 36 inches (91.4 cm) in Islamabad

Average Temperatures: 50°F (10°C) January, Islamabad; 90°F (32°C) July, Islamabad

Length of Coastline: 650 miles (1,046 km)

Greatest Distance North to South: 935 miles (1,505 km)

Greatest Distance East to West: 800 miles (1,287 km)

Major River: Indus River

Largest Natural Lake: Manchar Lake

Largest Artificial Lake: Keenjhar Lake

Largest Desert: Thar Desert

Highest Recorded Temperature: 127.4°F (53°C) at Jacobabad on June 12, 1919

Lowest Recorded Temperature: Information not available

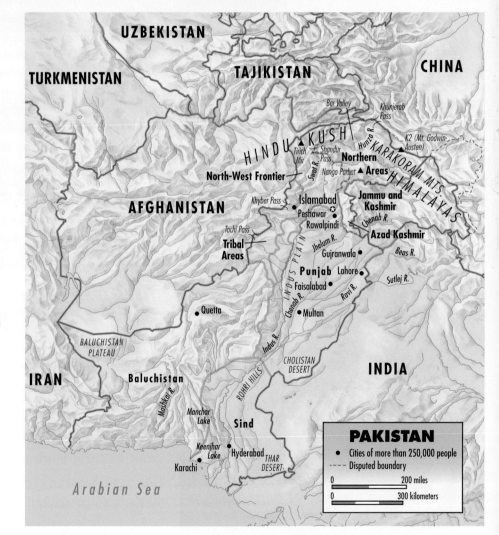

Pasu Glacier in northern Pakistan

A trekker stops to admire the mountains of the Karakoram range.

glaciers, or mountains of ice, rise among the mountains, too. Except for the earth's polar regions, Pakistan has the largest glaciers in the world. The runoff from the glaciers and snowy mountaintops feeds sparkling streams and bubbling waterfalls. Many clear, icy lakes nestle in the high valleys.

The Karakoram and Himalayan ranges run through Pakistan's Kashmir region. K2, in the Karakorams, is Pakistan's highest point. It is also the world's second-highest peak. Only Mount Everest, on the China–Nepal border, is higher. Nanga Parbat, in the Himalayas, is the world's ninth-highest peak. The Karakorams and the Himalayas gradually slope down to a high plateau. Here, much of the land is rough, rocky, and dry. Along Pakistan's northwest border with Afghanistan is the Hindu Kush range. Its highest peak is Tirich Mir.

More mountain ranges extend south from the Hindu Kush. They form much of Pakistan's western border with Afghanistan. Near the city of Peshawar is the famous Khyber Pass. This break in the mountains was the gateway for wave after wave of invasions. Today it is the major passage between Pakistan and Afghanistan. Politically, northwestern Pakistan is the country's North-West Frontier Province—one of Pakistan's four major divisions.

The Khyber Pass was once the entry point to Pakistan for invaders, but today it is used as the passageway between Pakistan and Afghanistan.

The Savage Mountain

K2, Pakistan's highest peak, has been called a savage mountain. That's because so many climbing expeditions on K2 have ended in disaster. Local people call it *Chogori*, meaning "King of Mountains." In 1856 a young British surveyor, T. G. Montgomerie, named the peak K2 when he was mapping the region. The "K" stands for "Karakorams," and it was the second mountain he mapped there. It is also called Mount Godwin-Austen after another surveyor, Henry Godwin-Austen, who climbed some of K2's glaciers and passes in 1860.

For almost a hundred years, one expedition after another struggled to reach its peak. All of them failed. They met with avalanches, blizzards, altitude sickness, frostbite, and food shortages. At last, in 1954, an Italian expedition made its way to the top.

High Mountain Valleys

The steep, narrow Bar Valley lies high in the Karakoram range. Soaring peaks and impressive glaciers rise in every direction. Mountain climbers as well as wildlife lovers are drawn to this valley. Scrambling along the mountainsides are Siberian ibex, a rare species of wild goat.

The Hunza River cuts through the Karakorams to create the Hunza Valley. The British explorer Eric Shipton called the valley "the ultimate manifestation of mountain grandeur." This valley is also said to be the inspiration for the legendary hidden valley of Shangri-La. It was made famous in James Hilton's novel *Lost Horizon*. In Hilton's Shangri-La, people lived for hundreds of years and never grew old.

The Hunza Valley, too, has dozens of glistening white glaciers and mountain peaks. Tribal dwellers in the valley raise crops on flourishing fields. In some areas they have cut terraces into the mountainsides so that they can farm on the steep slopes, too. Earlier civilizations left ancient rock carvings and the 600-year-old Baltit Castle.

The Swat River rushes through the rocky gorges of the Swat Valley. This valley gets abundant rainfall, so it's very lush and green, with many fruit-tree orchards and flower-covered slopes. Ancient forts and monasteries remain from earlier times. Today many villages are "stacked" up the mountainsides. The roofs on one level form a street for the houses above them.

Crops thrive on the terraced slopes of the Hunza Valley.

The Baluchistan Plateau

About midway down Pakistan's western border, the mountain chains change direction. From this point, they run almost directly south to the Arabian Sea. West of these mountains is a large region called the Baluchistan Plateau. It covers roughly the same area as Pakistan's Baluchistan Province.

This is the country's most sparsely populated region. The land is desolate, rocky, and very dry. However, it can be farmed using a centuries-old method of irrigation called the *karez*. It's a way of channeling water through underground tunnels to the fields. (See sidebar page 64.)

The Indus River flows between steep but fertile mountains.

The Indus Plain

The mighty Indus River begins high in the Himalayas, in Tibet, and runs south through all of Pakistan. Alongside the Indus is a broad lowland region called the Indus Plain. The northern part, or Upper Indus Plain, covers most of Pakistan's Punjab Province. This is Pakistan's most densely populated area. Islamabad, the capital city, is here, as are the big cities of Lahore, Rawalpindi, Faisalabad, and Multan.

Why is there such heavy settlement here? Because this is Pakistan's most fertile farming region. The Indus River's main tributaries flow through these plains. They are the Jhelum, Chenab, Ravi, Sutlej, and

Beas Rivers. In fact, those five rivers gave the Punjab its name. The word *Punjab* means "Five Waters." The lands between the rivers are called *doabs*. They are extensively irrigated with water from the rivers.

The Lower Indus Plain extends south along the Indus River to the Arabian Sea. It covers much of Pakistan's Sind Province. Near the mouth of the Indus is Karachi, Pakistan's largest city and major port. Farther upriver are Hyderabad and the ancient city of Mohenjo Daro.

The Indus River delta is a mass of channels that create a fanlike appearance.

Here on its southern course, the Indus often swells wide with waters from the north. Near its mouth, the Indus branches out into a fan-shaped delta. Some river deltas are fertile, but the Indus Delta is a wasteland, not fit for growing crops. When sea tides are high and the Indus swells, the delta becomes flooded. Manchar Lake, northwest of Karachi, is Pakistan's largest natural lake. It's hard to say exactly how big it is, though. It swells during the rainy season and shrinks in dry times.

Camels and their drovers rest on sand dunes in the Thar Desert, Pakistan's largest.

Deserts

Deserts cover many parts of eastern Pakistan. The Thar Desert extends over the border from India into southeastern Sind Province. It reaches into parts of the eastern Punjab, too. The Thar is Pakistan's largest desert region. Farmers there once raised only sheep. However, they can now cultivate crops in some areas through irrigation from the Punjab's rivers.

The Cholistan Desert spreads across southeastern Punjab. Dry winds sweep across the desert, whipping the sands into shifting waves and dunes. A few scattered villages are found there, but the soil is so dry and sandy that it's hard to raise any crops. People draw their water from underground wells. They make their way across the Cholistan by camel.

Climate

Pakistanis say they have three seasons—cool, hot, and wet. These seasons are very different in the northern mountains than in the southern plains. The cool season is Pakistan's winter. It lasts from about November through February. In the south, the days are mild and dry, and the nights are cool. But winters in the mountains can be bitterly cold, with freezing drizzle.

March through June is the hot season, or summer. Summers in the south are humid, and daytime temperatures can be sweltering. In the interior, away from the coast, summer days are blazing hot. On the other hand, summertime in the mountains is mild and pleasant.

The wet season—monsoon season—lasts from July through September. Monsoons, or torrential rains, sweep through all of southern Asia. This is when the Indus River has its worst floods. In October, once the monsoons are over, temperatures gradually begin to cool.

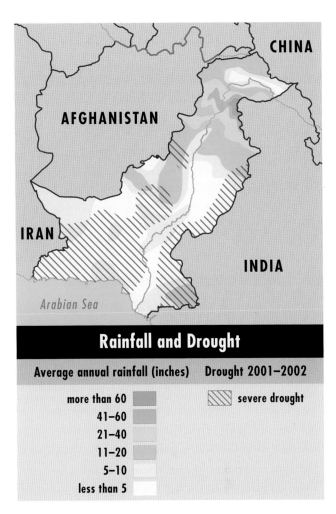

Rainfall and Drought

Average annual rainfall (inches)	Drought 2001–2002
more than 60	severe drought
41–60	
21–40	
11–20	
5–10	
less than 5	

In spite of its monsoon drenchings, Pakistan is generally quite dry. Very little rain falls in Baluchistan and the desert regions. And after the monsoons, the plains become dry again. Heavy rains fall on the lower slopes of the Himalayas. But most moisture in the mountains comes in the form of snow. Many of the high mountain regions are snow-covered all year round. As the weather warms, melting snow feeds the rivers.

Looking at Pakistan's Cities

Karachi (above) is Pakistan's largest city and the capital of Sind Province. It's located on the Arabian Sea shore near the mouth of the Indus River. Karachi was just a small fishing village until the 1700s. As its harbor developed, it grew into a prosperous center for industry and trade. Karachi was modern Pakistan's capital from 1947 to 1959. Today the city is a colorful blend of old and new. Its most famous landmark is the white-marble mausoleum of *Quaid-e-Azam* ("The Great Leader"). It is named for Muhammad Ali Jinnah, the Father of Pakistan. Visitors pay their respects there and watch the changing-of-the-guards ceremony. Another landmark is the huge mosque called Masjid-e-Tooba. Many bazaars line the streets of the old quarter, while modern shopping centers are in the newer areas. Vacationers enjoy Karachi's sunny beaches.

Lahore (opposite page) is Pakistan's second-largest city. It is the capital of Punjab Province and the nation's center for culture and learning. Beginning in the 1500s, Lahore was the Mughal Empire's cultural center.

Today the city is a showcase for beautiful Mughal buildings. They include Badshahi Mosque, the Royal Fort, the tombs of Emperor Jahangir and the poet Allama Iqbal, and the Shalimar Gardens complex. Lahore's Walled City section contains many centuries-old buildings. The modern Minar-e-Pakistan tower honors the 1940 resolution to create a separate state for Muslims in British India—the future Pakistan.

Faisalabad is Pakistan's third-largest city, famous for its textile industry. Faisalabad's centerpiece is Ghanta Ghar Bazaar. The city used to be called Lyallpur, after the Punjab's British governor Sir Charles James Lyall.

Rawalpindi is the fourth-largest city and the "twin city" of neighboring Islamabad, the capital. Rawalpindi was Pakistan's capital from 1959 to 1969. A culture flourished in this region as far back as 3,000 years. It was an early Buddhist center, and the second-century Mangklala Stupa (shrine) remains from that time. A Muslim Gakkhar chief, Jhanda Khan, named the city Rawalpindi in 1493. Sikhs took over in 1765, then the British seized the city in 1849, making it the army's general headquarters. The Old City and its bazaars still have a traditional flavor.

Multan is an ancient city, with many historic sites and monuments. Among its conquerors were Alexander the Great around 326 B.C., Muhammad bin Qasim in 712, and Timur (Tamerlane) in 1398. Many Muslim saints and scholars lived in Multan. Their shrines include the mausoleum of Rukn-e-Alam. Its dome is one of the largest in the world.

Peshawar lies at the foot of the historic Khyber Pass. Many invaders marched through this break in the mountains on their conquests. They included Aryans, Greeks, Huns, and the Mughal emperor Babur. Today Peshawar is the capital of the North-West Frontier Province and the center of the Pathan tribal region.

Traders, craftsmen, and shopkeepers line the Old City's narrow streets. Rifle-bearing tribesmen and horse-drawn carts pass by. The Mughal mosque of Mahabat Khan and the massive Balahisaar Fort are some of Peshawar's landmarks.

Quetta is the capital of Baluchistan Province. Its people are mainly Pathan, Baloch, and Brahui tribes-people. High mountains surround Quetta, and nomadic herders pass through on their seasonal migrations. The Quetta region is known for its fruits. Farmers there grow plums, peaches, pomegranates, and apples, as well as pistachios and almonds. Quetta's bazaars are famous for their mirror-work embroidery. Near the city is Hazarganji-Chiltan National Park. It is a haven for the markhor, a wild goat that is Pakistan's national animal.

(For Islamabad see page 61.)

Animal and Plant Communities

PAKISTAN'S LANDSCAPES RANGE FROM MARSHY SEACOASTS to arid deserts to high mountain peaks. They provide homes for many types of wildlife. Each region has its own ecosystems, or plant and animal communities. Within each ecosystem all the species interact and depend on one another. Some of the world's rarest plants and animals live in Pakistan. Unfortunately, many of them are in danger of losing their habitats.

Pakistan's rate of deforestation, or forest clearing, is one of the highest in the world. As forests are lost, so too are the animals and the plants that depend on them. Overgrazing and soil erosion are other threats to the wildlife.

The good news is that Pakistan has many protected areas. They include fourteen national parks, ninety-nine wildlife sanctuaries, and ninety-six game reserves. Pakistan has a Biodiversity Action Plan, too. Its purpose is to protect the country's wildlife. The government is also involving local people in conservation.

Opposite: **A shepherd and his herd cross the Shyok River.**

Kirthar National Park

Kirthar National Park, northeast of Karachi, is Pakistan's oldest national park. It's home to several rare and threatened animal species. They include the urial sheep, the chinkara gazelle, and the Sind ibex, a wild goat. Jungle cats, Asiatic leopards, and wolves prowl there, too.

Beautiful wildflowers bloom during the late-summer monsoons. The park also contains several important archaeological sites. Environmentalists are worried about Kirthar's future, especially because oil companies are hoping to drill for oil and natural gas there.

Alpine forests thrive on the hills in the North-West Frontier Province.

Diverse Plant Zones

Pakistan's mountains and hills have many types of plants. Alpine forests grow high in the mountains. Their fir and juniper trees are dwarfed and stunted because the air has so little oxygen. At lower elevations are forests of cone-bearing trees, or conifers. They include fir, spruce, pine, and juniper trees. Here, too, grow cedar trees called deodars, the national tree. The foothills of the mountains are covered with deciduous trees—that is, trees that shed their leaves in the winter. Grasses cover the high meadows, and the rainy season brings out a dazzling show of wildflowers.

Subtropical plants grow on the dry, hilly areas of the Baluchistan, Punjab, and North-West Frontier provinces.

Acacias are very common trees there. Their thorns help to hold moisture in the dry climate. Other thorny trees and shrubs grow across the dry, sandy plains. So do tough, wiry grasses.

Narrow strips of forest grow along the banks of the Indus and its tributaries. In the irrigated regions, farmers introduced many trees in the 1800s. Some of these transplants are mulberry, eucalyptus, and poplar trees. Mangrove trees grow in the marshy Indus Delta.

Poplar trees grow well near terraced farmland.

The National Tree and Flower

The deodar cedar is Pakistan's national tree. It's popularly known as the royal tree. Huge deodar trunks were used as roof beams in many of Pakistan's centuries-old shrines. The deodar's branches form a pyramid shape, and its light red wood is still valuable as timber.

The jasmine (pictured) is Pakistan's national flower. It's a small, white flower whose fragrance is heavy and sweet, and its oil is used as a perfume. The jasmine has often been used as a romantic symbol in Persian and Arabic poetry. Jasmine, or Yasmin, is a popular girl's name in Pakistan and other countries in the region. Jasmine grows abundantly in Lahore, a city known for its beautiful gardens. Many varieties of jasmine grow in Islamabad's Rose and Jasmine Garden.

Birds and Water Creatures

Birds of prey, such as the golden eagle, are a common sight in Pakistan.

Many large birds of prey soar through the skies over Pakistan. There are golden eagles, vultures, falcons, kestrels, and sparrow hawks. Some of Pakistan's smaller birds are bulbuls, flycatchers, pheasants, orioles, larks, doves, and partridges.

Many water birds live in Pakistan's wetlands, and thousands of birds descend on these wetlands during their migrations. Manchar Lake is home to spoonbills, pelicans, wood ducks, mallards, and other birds. Lake Haleji, near Karachi, is an official wetland bird sanctuary. Flamingos, egrets, kingfishers, and Hubara bustards are some other common birds.

The National Bird

The chukar partridge is Pakistan's national bird. Mostly gray, it has a black band across its eyes and black bars across the sides of its belly. Its bill and legs are bright red. This hardy bird lives in Pakistan's dry and semi-arid mountain regions. The larger Himalayan snowcock is sometimes called its giant cousin.

Due to hunting, pollution, and beach development, green sea turtles are in need of protection by wildlife agencies in Pakistan.

Crocodiles, wild boars, and pythons slink through the mangrove swamps of the Indus Delta. Giant sea turtles nest along the seacoast near Karachi. They come ashore to lay their eggs in September. The main species are the green turtle and the olive ridley turtle. Both species are in trouble. Some are hunted for their shells and skins, and others are accidentally caught in fishing nets. Pollution, beach development, and wild dogs are also constant threats. Pakistan's wildlife agencies are working with local communities to protect the turtles.

The Indus River dolphin is one of the world's rarest mammals. A scant few hundred exist, and they live only in the Indus and its tributaries. This dolphin is said to be blind. It does have eyes, but the eyes have no lenses. Scientists are not sure what benefit these dolphins get from their eyes. They may be able to perceive light, and this would help them find direction. The government of Sind Province established the Indus River Dolphin Reserve in 1974. Most of the existing dolphin population lives there, and they are protected from fishing.

Asiatic black bears live on the forested mountainsides. They are black, with a white patch of fur on their chest. They eat insects, fruit, and small animals. Their forest homes are shrinking as loggers cut the trees down. Hunters, too, reduce their population. In some Asian countries, bear paws are an expensive, exotic food. The bears' gall bladders are a prized ingredient in traditional Chinese medicine.

A mountain dweller, the Asiatic black bear, lives on ants, small animals, fruit, and seeds.

Other mountain creatures are brown bears, wild sheep and goats, and barking deer. Deosai Plains National Park, in the Himalaya and Karakoram region, protects Pakistan's largest colony of brown bears, though it has only about two dozen bears. Some of the country's smaller animals are golden marmots, hamsters, porcupines, jackals, foxes, and pikas, a short-eared, rabbitlike mammal.

Pakistan is the only place in the world where the woolly flying squirrel lives. Wildlife watchers once thought it was extinct. Now, however, these plump squirrels have been found in the northern mountains.

Sand cats live in Pakistan's rocky desert areas. They are small, short-legged cats with big ears. Thick hair grows between the pads of their feet. They feed on small reptiles, rodents, and birds. A larger wildcat is the caracal, which lives in dry mountain regions. Caracals have long legs, a short tail, and no spots. They prey on antelopes as well as on birds and rodents. The beautiful spotted Asiatic cheetah may be extinct in the wild in Pakistan; however, rumors of sightings have raised hopes that it still exists.

Sand cats are among the smallest wildcats. They are about the size of domestic cats.

The National Animal

The flare-horned markhor, a wild goat, is Pakistan's national animal. Its majestic horns curve in wide spirals that measure up to 5 feet (1.5 meters) across. That makes the markhor a prized trophy for hunters. They are found in mountain regions that have a dry temperate climate. That includes parts of the Northern Areas and the Chitral and Swat areas. They eat leaves and grass and they have even been known to climb trees to munch on their leaves. A related species is the straight-horned markhor. Both species are endangered. Now protected in several national parks, the markhor are increasing in number.

Saving the Snow Leopards

One of Pakistan's most exotic creatures is the rare snow leopard. Snow leopards are found in China and Mongolia to the east, and throughout Pakistan and Afghanistan. In Pakistan they prowl the jagged rocks and cliffs of the northern mountains. They have a whitish spotted coat, pale blue eyes, and a tuft on the end of their tail. Their large paw pads help them grip the rocks as they leap across deep ravines.

Snow leopards prey on other wild animals. However, their natural quarry is getting scarce, as tribal mountain people in remote regions hunt the same animals. As a result, snow leopards sometimes attack tribesmen's yaks, horses, or goats. Herders may trap or shoot leopards to protect their herds. Poachers, or illegal hunters, are another threat. They hunt snow leopards for their skins and bones. The thick, furry skins can fetch a price many times higher than a villager's yearly income. The bones are used in traditional Chinese medicine.

A new conservation project is helping to protect the snow leopards, and the mountain people themselves are involved. Encouraged by the World Wildlife Fund, tribespeople in the Bar Valley manage this community project. They agreed to stop hunting the leopards' natural prey, such as wild sheep and goats, and to act as guards to protect them. Snow leopards now have plenty of wild game to hunt, so they do not need to attack the domestic herds. As the wild game population grows, the tribespeople allow hunters in, charging them hefty fees. So far this experiment has worked in a few locations. Wildlife watchdogs are hoping to involve more communities in the future.

The snow leopard population has been declining, but through conservation efforts their numbers can be expected to increase.

Ancient Kingdoms and a Modern Nation

ANCIENT PAKISTAN WAS HOME TO SOME OF THE OLDEST civilizations on earth. Archaeologists have dug up amazing ruins and art objects from the past. Tools found in the Siwalik Hills near Rawalpindi may be 500,000 years old. Rock paintings in the Rohri Hills near Jacobabad are at least 25,000 years old. The Mehrgarh civilization of Baluchistan arose in the 7000s B.C. Its people built mud-brick homes, grew wheat and barley, and raised cattle.

Opposite: **The Chaukundi Tombs were built during the sixteenth to eighteenth centuries by the Baluchi and Burpat tribes.**

The Indus Valley Civilization

By about 2500 B.C., people in the Indus Valley had developed an advanced way of life. The Indus civilization flourished at the same time as civilizations in ancient Egypt and Mesopotamia (present-day Iraq).

The major cities in the Indus Valley were Harappa and Mohenjo Daro. They had a highly organized government system, and they built huge stone buildings and monuments. Larger homes even had indoor plumbing, complete with bathrooms and drainpipes. Merchants used a standard system of weights and measures. The people had a writing system, too. Seals, or small stone slabs, were intricately carved with writings and pictures of animals. No one knows why

This Indus civilization seal dates from about 2500–1700 B.C.

the Indus civilization began to decline around 1700 B.C. However, archaelogists have found signs of floods, economic hardship, and overcrowding of cities.

Aryan people from central Asia arrived around 1500 B.C. They were a nomadic people who spoke an Indo-European language. They settled in the Punjab and continued to spread throughout most of India. The Aryans' Vedic religion was the ancestor of Hinduism. Their scriptures are called the *Vedas*, which means "knowledge" in Sanskrit. These collections of religious verses and prayers were originally passed down by word of mouth.

Mohenjo Daro

Mohenjo Daro was once the largest city of the Indus Valley Civilization. Its name means "Mound of the Dead." This ancient city lies on the west bank of the Indus River in Sind. Its highest point was a religious and ceremonial center, with assembly halls, luxurious homes, a massive grain storehouse, and a large public bath. On lower ground were middle-class homes. Most were built around courtyards and had bathrooms. One famous artifact found at Mohenjo Daro is a bronze dancing girl. Stone seals and terra-cotta figurines of bulls have been found, too.

UNESCO (the United Nations Educational, Scientific, and Cultural Organization) has declared

Mohenjo Daro a World Heritage site. That means it is to be protected as a site of great value to all the world's people.

Invasions and Empires

The next centuries brought many more invasions. Persians arrived in the 500s B.C. with Cyrus the Great. In 327 B.C. Alexander the Great brought his Greek and Macedonian armies into the region. They fought their way across the Punjab. But when they reached the Beas River, the army refused to go on. Some historians believe they were afraid of the fierce warriors with armies of elephants that they had heard were beyond the river.

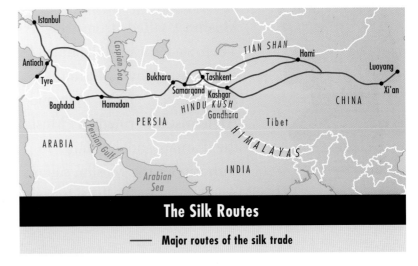

The Silk Routes

— Major routes of the silk trade

The Gandhara region was an important crossroads for both invaders and traders. It lay just east of the Khyber Pass, surrounding Peshawar. Under the Mauryan Empire (c. 321–185 B.C.), which followed Alexander the Great, Gandhara became a center for the Buddhist religion. Taxila and Peshawar were Gandhara's main cultural centers.

The Kushan dynasty arose in the first century A.D. From their capital near Peshawar, the Kushans ruled a vast empire. It spread from Afghanistan through Pakistan into northern India. The greatest Kushan king was Kaniska. He made Buddhism the empire's official religion. Kushan kings built many Buddhist monasteries, temples, and stone

statues of the Buddha (Siddhartha Gautama). Gandhara became a center for Buddhist study and devotion. It was also the center for the Silk Route trade between China and India to the east and Arabia and the Roman Empire to the west.

The religion of Islam entered Pakistan in A.D. 711, when Muslims sailed from the Arabian Peninsula to Sind. Their leader was Muhammad bin Qasim. Over the following centuries, many Muslim kingdoms would rule Pakistan. Around A.D. 1000 Mahmud of Ghazna, in present-day Afghanistan, ruled a Muslim kingdom that included the Punjab and Kashmir. In 1206 Pakistan fell under the authority of the Muslim sultans, or rulers, of Delhi in northern India. The Delhi sultanate remained in power for more than 300 years.

Gandharan statue of the Buddha

Babur and the Mughal Emperors

Babur (1483–1530) (pictured) was a descendant of two great central Asian warriors—Genghis Khan and Timur. Babur, whose name means "tiger," invaded Pakistan in 1526. By 1529 he had conquered India and established the great Mughal Empire.

Babur's son Humayan ruled next, and then his son, Akbar, reigned from 1556 to 1605. Akbar created a highly organized government throughout the empire. Akbar's son Jahangir ruled from 1605 to 1627. He was known as a patron of the arts, favoring Persian styles. Jahangir's son Shah Jahan reigned from 1628 to 1658. He built many beautiful monuments. The best known is India's magnificent Taj Mahal, a memorial to his wife. Shah Jahan's son Aurangzeb was emperor from 1658 until his death in 1707. Great Britain ousted the last Mughal emperor in the mid-1800s.

The Mughal Empire

Babur was a Muslim prince from central Asia. In 1526 he marched his armies across the Hindu Kush and by 1529 had established the great Mughal Empire. This vast kingdom stretched across present-day India, Pakistan, Bangladesh, and Afghanistan. Its culture was a blend of Hindu Indian and Muslim Persian elements. Arts, architecture, and literature flourished under the Mughals. The Urdu language also developed at this time. Today Urdu is Pakistan's official language.

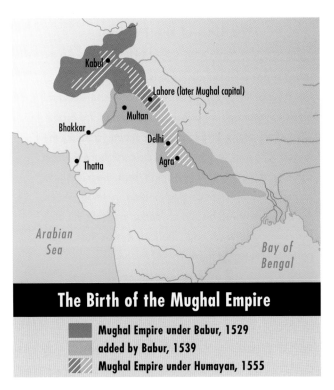

The Birth of the Mughal Empire

Mughal Empire under Babur, 1529
added by Babur, 1539
Mughal Empire under Humayan, 1555

Meanwhile, Europeans had their eye on the region's valuable trade routes. Dutch, Portuguese, French, and British trading companies made deals with the Mughal leaders. Often the traders gained a foothold through vicious attacks. Soon there were European trading colonies all along India's coast.

By the 1700s, Mughal emperors were losing a grip on their vast empire. Local kings and princes were gaining much more power than the emperors. One powerful leader was Ranjit Singh, a member of the Sikh religion. Sikhism, with elements of both Hinduism and Islam, had been growing in the region since the 1500s. Ranjit Singh became the maharajah, or prince, of Lahore in 1799 and built an empire across the Indus Valley.

The Lion of the Punjab

Ranjit Singh (1780–1839) was a Sikh ruler who established a powerful kingdom. He is known as the Lion of the Punjab. In 1799 he seized Lahore and declared himself maharajah, or prince, of the Punjab. He gradually added more territories to his realm, creating the largest kingdom in the Indus Valley. Afghans were a constant threat, but Ranjit Singh kept them out. He helped the British invade Afghanistan in 1838. When the British removed his son as leader in 1849, the Sikh kingdom came to an end. The Punjab was then incorporated with British India.

British India and the Muslims

By this time, the British East India Company had edged out its trading competitors. As the Mughal Empire weakened, the British saw their chance to grab more than just trade. Little by little, they gained political control of the Indian subcontinent.

Kashmir fell under British control in 1846. For the British, this region was a "buffer state" against Russia to the northwest. By 1849 the British controlled Sind and the Punjab. All these lands, together with present-day India and Bangladesh, were called British India. They made up just one colony of the far-flung British Empire.

Muslims in British India had a hard time knowing where they stood. Muslim rulers had dominated India since the 1200s. Yet the majority of Indians were Hindus. Muslim people were scattered throughout India. They were especially numerous in the northwest (present-day Pakistan) and in East

Bengal (present-day Bangladesh). But once the Mughal Empire fell, Muslims found themselves simply a minority group.

Indians formed the Indian National Congress in 1885. It pushed for independence from Great Britain. Although Muslims were involved in this movement, the Hindu majority dominated it. Muslims began to realize that, if British India became independent, Muslims would have no real voice in the government. In 1906 Muslims formed the All-India Muslim League. In time the league began to call for a separate Muslim state.

Among Muslim leaders, no one worked harder *against* separation than Muhammad Ali Jinnah. He spent years working toward cooperation between Muslims and Hindus. Yet as a new Indian government took shape, Muslims were shut out

In 1946 members of the All-India Muslim League demonstrated in London for the partition of India and the creation of the state of Pakistan.

The Great Leader

Muhammad Ali Jinnah (1876–1948) is called the Father of Pakistan. He is also known as *Quaid-e-Azam*, which means "The Great Leader." Born in Karachi and educated in London, Jinnah became a distinguished lawyer. He served in the Indian National Congress and became president of the All-India Muslim League. Until the mid-1930s Jinnah strongly believed that Hindus and Muslims should work together to form a unified India. However, he began to realize that Muslims would not have much of a voice in India's government. In time, he convinced the All-India Muslim League, the Indian National Congress, and the British government that India would have to be divided. Jinnah became Pakistan's first governor-general in 1947. He died only a year later.

time and again. Bloody riots broke out between Hindu and Muslim communities across India. In the end, even Jinnah realized that the only hope was a separate Muslim state.

Badshah Khan

Abdul Ghaffar Khan (1890–1988) was a great Pashtun leader. He was born near Peshawar, the son of a tribal chief. Brilliant and strong, he was offered a military position and a university education by the British. Instead, as a devout Muslim, he chose to travel among rural Pashtun villages preaching hard work and self-sacrifice. He also worked to set up schools for Pashtun children. His people called him *Badshah Khan*, meaning "Khan of Khans" or "King of Kings."

Ghaffar Khan developed a close relationship with Mahatma Gandhi, the Hindu leader who led India's struggle for independence. Like Gandhi, he preached nonviolent resistance and civil disobedience. He also shared Gandhi's desire for Muslims and Hindus to work together. Thus he was often called the Frontier Gandhi.

In 1929 Ghaffar Khan founded a nonviolent movement called *Khudai Khidmatgar*, meaning "Servants of God." It was dedicated to social reform and to the end of British rule through nonviolence. The British killed and imprisoned hundreds of its members. Ghaffar Khan himself was imprisoned for more than thirty years. Even in his nineties, he continued to work for human rights, mutual respect, and nonviolent solutions to problems.

Pakistan—the Idea and the Name

Allama Muhammad Iqbal (1877–1938) was a poet and philosopher who wrote verses in both Persian and Urdu. He was also involved in politics, and in 1930 he became the first person to suggest the idea of a Muslim state. Iqbal believed this state should consist of India's four northwestern provinces. At that time, they were the Punjab, Sind, Baluchistan, and the North-West Frontier—Pakistan's four provinces today.

In 1933 a Muslim university student suggested the name *Pakstan*. Each of the first four letters of the word stood for a region where Muslims lived—Punjab, Afghan (the North-West Frontier Province), Kashmir, and Sind. The end of "Baluchistan" provided the end of the word.

The new nation's name eventually became *Pakistan*, "Land of the Pure."

Division and Independence

Independence came at last in 1947, after much fighting and disorder. The subcontinent was partitioned into two parts. The large central section became the country of India. The Muslim country consisted of two sections—West Pakistan and East Pakistan. West Pakistan was made up of India's four northwestern provinces. East Pakistan was a smaller area to the southeast. It had been part of India's Bengal Province. The two territories were more than 1,000 miles (1,609 kilometers) apart.

As for Jammu and Kashmir, it wanted to remain independent. Its people were mostly Muslim, while its ruling prince was Hindu. Both Pakistan and India believed they had reason to claim it. The two countries

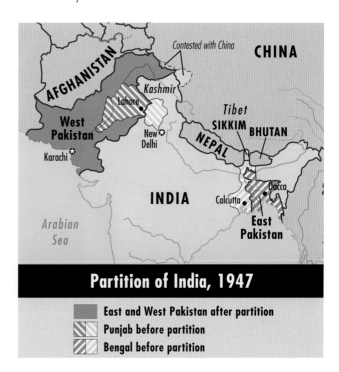

Partition of India, 1947

- East and West Pakistan after partition
- Punjab before partition
- Bengal before partition

fought over Jammu and Kashmir until the United Nations (UN) stepped in in 1949. To resolve the issue, at least for a while, the UN ruled that both India and Pakistan would govern a part of the region.

Decades of Turmoil

Pakistanis welcomed Muhammad Ali Jinnah as their first head of state. Unfortunately, he died after only a year in office. Then warring political parties kept the country in turmoil. Pakistan drew up a constitution and proclaimed itself an Islamic republic in 1956. But General Muhammad Ayub Khan took over in 1958. He put Pakistan under martial law, or military rule; then in 1960 he was elected president. Under Ayub Khan, Pakistan fought a war with India over Kashmir in 1965, which ended in a cease-fire.

West Pakistan's economy grew in the 1960s, but relations with East Pakistan were crumbling. After a civil war East Pakistan declared its independence in 1971. It took the name Bangladesh, meaning "Land of the Bengals." Now West Pakistan became simply "Pakistan."

Zulfikar Ali Bhutto came to power in 1971. He had opposed both peace with India and the division of Pakistan. Bhutto was a popular leader,

Zulfikar Ali Bhutto, Pakistani leader from 1971 to 1977

but General Mohammad Zia-ul-Haq deposed him in 1977 and executed him. Zia-ul-Haq pleased religious conservatives with his policy of "Islamization." It made the observation of strict Islamic law the guiding force in Pakistan's legal system. He was killed in 1988 when his airplane exploded in midair.

Bhutto's daughter, Benazir Bhutto, became prime minister in 1988. She was the first woman to be elected leader of a Muslim country. However, her government came under fire for corruption. Her opponent Muhammad Nawaz Sharif became prime minister in 1997.

General Pervez Musharraf staged a military takeover in 1999. As his reasons, he pointed to Pakistan's lagging economy, high crime rate, and corruption. Musharraf suspended Pakistan's constitution and legislature. In June 2001 he declared himself president and enacted changes in the constitution. Elections were held in 2002 that returned Pakistan to civilian rule.

General Mohammad Zia-ul-Haq led Pakistan under strict Islamic law.

Afghanistan and the War on Terrorism

Meanwhile, Pakistan's neighbor Afghanistan had been in turmoil since the 1970s. Military leaders had taken over its government in 1978, but Afghan rebels tried to overthrow the military government. The Soviet Union, siding with the military, invaded to fight the rebels. Pakistan, the United States, and other countries aided the rebels. At last, in 1989, the Soviet Union withdrew.

Peace did not descend on Afghanistan, though. A group called the Taliban won control in 1996. Many of them had grown up in refugee camps in Pakistan. The Taliban enforced an extreme, often violent control over their country. They also allowed the international terrorist group al-Qaeda to train in Afghanistan. On September 11, 2001, al-Qaeda terrorists took control of several U.S. passenger planes, killing thousands. Two planes crashed into the World Trade Center towers in New York City, destroying both buildings. Another plane severely damaged the Pentagon building outside Washington, D.C. A fourth plane was downed in Pennsylvania. The United States and its allies launched a campaign against terrorism in response.

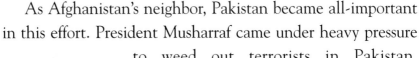

Pakistani police officers escort three Islamic militants into an antiterrorism court in Karachi.

As Afghanistan's neighbor, Pakistan became all-important in this effort. President Musharraf came under heavy pressure to weed out terrorists in Pakistan. Pakistan's army had aided the Taliban back in the "rebel days" of the 1980s. Many extremists and army officers in Pakistan still sided with the Taliban and al-Qaeda.

As the country's military leader, Musharraf had a tough decision to make. He decided to take a firm stance against terrorism. He had many suspected terrorists arrested and helped the United States

investigate terrorist networks. That remains a tough battle. In 2002 Pakistani terrorists kidnapped and killed an American journalist. Bombings and killings in Pakistan's Christian communities also occurred.

An Uncertain Future

Throughout Afghanistan's years of warfare, more than 3 million Afghan refugees fled to Pakistan. These newcomers put a strain on the country's resources. They needed food, shelter, and other basic necessities. International aid groups helped, but the refugees still competed with Pakistanis for living space, food, and fuel.

Pakistan and India continued to clash over Kashmir in the early 2000s. The two countries almost went to war over the region in 2002. Since both nations have nuclear weapons, countries around the world were alarmed at the destruction they could cause.

Pakistan's industries are growing, but its economy is still weak. Much of the population is very poor. Extreme religious values govern much of Pakistani life. However, this trend is growing weaker. The world community hopes that the future may bring more freedoms and a better life for all Pakistanis.

Hundreds of Afghan refugees wait in hope of receiving relief goods and aid.

The Struggle for Democracy

PAKISTAN'S OFFICIAL NAME IS THE ISLAMIC REPUBLIC OF Pakistan. Its first constitution made it a republic with a parliamentary form of government. Most of Great Britain's former colonies adopted this same system. Many conflicts have challenged Pakistan's political system, though. Political parties often opposed one another fiercely. At other times, the military clashed with civilian officials.

In some way all these conflicts are struggles for democracy. They are fights for equal rights among all Pakistanis. That includes rich and poor, religious and secular, city people and rural groups.

Opposite: **Men raising the Pakistani flag in Lahore.**

Qazi Hussain Ahmed, chief of Pakistan's religious political party, addresses a public meeting in the city of Charsada.

The National Flag

Pakistan's national flag features a white crescent moon and a five-pointed star against a dark green background. Along the left edge is a white band. The moon and star are traditional symbols of Islam. For Pakistan, the crescent also represents progress, while the star stands for light and knowledge. Green is Islam's traditional color. On the flag, the green area stands for the Muslim majority, while the white band represents Pakistan's minority groups. This flag was designed by Muhammad Ali Jinnah, a founder of Pakistan. It was adopted in 1947 after partition.

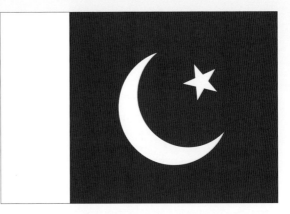

"Qaumi Tarana" ("National Anthem")

Adopted in 1954
Words by Hafiz Jalandhari; music by Ahmed Ghulamali Chagla

Blessed be the sacred land,
Happy be the bounteous realm,
Symbol of high resolve,
Land of Pakistan.
Blessed be thou citadel of faith.

The order of this sacred land
Is the might of the brotherhood of the people.
May the nation, the country, and the state
Shine in glory everlasting.
Blessed be the goal of our ambition.

This flag of crescent and the star
Leads the way to progress and perfection,
Interpreter of our past, glory of our present,
Inspiration of our future,
Symbol of the Almighty's protection.

Pakistanis lived under military regimes several times in their recent history—1958–1971, 1977–1978, and 1999–2002. General Pervez Musharraf ushered in yet another military regime in 1999. Each time, the usual government systems were dissolved, either partly or completely.

Who will govern Pakistan? This question has kept the country in turmoil since its birth. Still, certain basic democratic structures remain—either in memory or as earnest ideal.

The Constitution

Pakistan adopted its first constitution in 1956. However, severe conflicts soon broke out among various regions and political

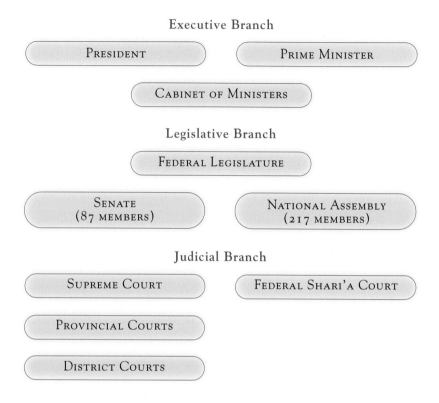

NATIONAL GOVERNMENT OF PAKISTAN

Executive Branch

PRESIDENT   PRIME MINISTER

CABINET OF MINISTERS

Legislative Branch

FEDERAL LEGISLATURE

SENATE
(87 MEMBERS)   NATIONAL ASSEMBLY
(217 MEMBERS)

Judicial Branch

SUPREME COURT   FEDERAL SHARI'A COURT

PROVINCIAL COURTS

DISTRICT COURTS

parties. The government ground to a halt. In 1958 the constitution was revoked under martial law. A new constitution in 1962 gave local governors a lot of power. A third constitution was adopted in 1973 but suspended in 1977. That constitution was restored with amendments, or changes, in 1985.

The constitution called for a president and a prime minister, who make up the executive branch of government. It also provided for a two-chamber legislature, or parliament, as the lawmaking body. Each of the four provinces has its own provincial assembly.

Executive Powers

Officially, Pakistan's president is the head of state. That is the person who represents Pakistan among other national leaders throughout the world. The prime minister is the head of the government. He or she oversees the government's operations within the country. Both officers must be Muslims. According to the constitution, the president is to be chosen by an electoral college. This group consists of the national legislature and the provincial assemblies. The president's term lasts five years. He or she is to act on the advice of the prime minister.

Pakistan's president has sometimes had far-reaching powers. Traditionally, the National Assembly elects the prime minister. But as of 1985 the president could appoint the prime minister. That measure was repealed in 1997. In 1999 the military government shifted the balance of power once again.

Pervez Musharraf

Pervez Musharraf was born in New Delhi, India, in 1943. When Pakistan separated from India, his family moved to Karachi. Musharraf's father was a diplomat, and the family lived in Turkey from 1949 to 1956. Musharraf was appointed head of Pakistan's armed forces in 1998. The following year he deposed Prime Minister Nawaz Sharif and declared himself chief executive. He became president in 2001. In a 2002 national referendum, or vote of the people's opinion, he was elected president for a five-year term. Musharraf cracked down on terrorists after Afghanistan's Taliban government fell in 2001. He also worked to reduce the power of Islamic extremists in Pakistan's government.

Executive power would rest in the hands of a National Security Council, headed by a chief executive. Under this system, there is no prime minister.

The Legislature

The legislature, or parliament, is called the Majlis-e-Shoora. That's derived from an Arabic term for a council of advisers. The *majlis* is an old tradition in Islamic communities. Pakistan's legislature has two chambers, or houses. The lower house is the National Assembly, with 217 members. Of those, 207 seats are reserved for Muslims, and the other 10 are for non-Muslims. Members are chosen by direct vote of the people and serve five-year terms.

The upper chamber is the Senate. Its eighty-seven members are chosen by the assemblies in the provinces. Senators serve six-year terms. Every two years, one-third of the Senate seats are up for election. In most cases, the Senate's role is to advise the National Assembly. Sometimes the Senate disagrees with a law passed by the Assembly. In that case, the Senate can send the law back for the Assembly to reconsider it. However, the Senate may do this only once for each law.

Prime minister Zafarullah Khan Jamali speaks in the Parliament in Islamabad.

Benazir Bhutto

Benazir Bhutto was born in Karachi in 1953. She was educated at Harvard University in the United States and Oxford University in England. Bhutto was the first female leader of a Muslim country in modern times. She served two terms as Pakistan's prime minister—1988 to 1990 and 1993 to 1996. Her father, Zulfikar Ali Bhutto, founded the Pakistan People's Party (PPP) and was prime minister in the 1970s. After his execution in 1979, Benazir became the PPP's leader. When her party won a majority of National Assembly seats in the 1988 elections, she became prime minister. Muhammad Nawaz Sharif, her opponent in the Islamic Democratic Alliance (IDL) and the Pakistan Muslim League (PML) parties, served after each of her two terms.

Muhammad Nawaz Sharif

Muhammad Nawaz Sharif was Pakistan's prime minister from 1990 to 1993 and from 1997 to 1999. When first elected, Sharif was the leader of the Islamic Democratic Alliance (IDL) party. It was an alliance of several Islamic and other groups. Later he headed the Nawaz branch of the Pakistan Muslim League (PML) party. Sharif had also been chief minister of the Punjab. In 1999 General Pervez Musharraf deposed Sharif.

The Law Courts in Lahore

The Courts and the Legal System

Pakistan's highest court is the Supreme Court. Beneath the Supreme Court are the high courts of each province. These courts, in turn, oversee district courts.

Pakistan's laws originally grew out of British common law. Common law simply means laws that developed over the years as cases came up and judicial decisions were made. To this base Pakistan added Islamic elements. Religious conservatives have always had a strong voice in Pakistani politics. Some want Pakistan's laws to be more in line with *shari'a*, or Islamic law. Others insist that shari'a be made Pakistan's *only* code of laws.

In 1979 General Zia introduced certain criminal punishments called for under Islamic law. They included whippings, stonings, and amputations for serious crimes. However, Zia did not adopt full shari'a. The next year a federal shari'a court was established. It was to decide whether any law was contrary to Islamic law. In 1998 the National Assembly passed an amendment replacing Pakistan's legal codes with full shari'a. However, the Senate did not approve it.

Local Divisions and Provincial Governments

Pakistan is divided into four provinces. They are the Punjab, Sind, Baluchistan, and the North-West Frontier. Another division is the Islamabad Capital Territory.

Each of the four provinces has a provincial governor, a chief minister, a provincial assembly, and provincial high courts. Each province is also divided into smaller districts. Pakistan's president appoints the provincial governors. From time to time military regimes have suspended provincial governments. The president also appoints an administrator to govern the capital territory. This person has the same powers as a provincial governor.

Yet another division is the Federally Administered Tribal Areas (FATA). There are seven main tribal areas—Khyber, Kurram, Orakzai, Mohmand, Bajaur, North Waziristan, and South Waziristan. They are clustered along Pakistan's western border with Afghanistan. The people who live there are ethnic Pashtuns. Four other tribal areas are scattered within the North-West Frontier Province. Officially, Pakistan's president governs the tribal areas. But tribal elders, called *maliks*, have authority over most day-to-day affairs.

Pakistan also governs Azad Kashmir and the Northern Areas. A national government agency oversees both regions. Azad Kashmir has its own local government, too.

Islamabad: Did You Know This?

Islamabad was chosen to be Pakistan's capital in 1959. After years of construction, it became the official capital in 1969. Previous capitals had been Karachi (1947–1959) and Islamabad's neighboring city of Rawalpindi (1959–1969). The city itself lies within the federal capital territory. The name *Islamabad* means "City of Islam" or "City of Peace."

Islamabad was built to reflect both tradition and a modern outlook. It is divided into several zones for different activities, such as government (above), industry, and residences. Government buildings include the Secretariat, Pakistan House (President's House), and the National Assembly Building. One zone is a park with an Olympic village, gardens, and farms. Other structures are the Shah Faisal Mosque, the Quaid-i-Azam University, and Alama Iqbal Open University. The Margala Hills rise over Islamabad to the north and northeast.

Founded: 1959

Location: Potwar Plateau, northeast Pakistan

Number of districts: 8

City population: 524,500 (1998 census)

Capital territory population: 799,000 (1998 census)

City area: 25 square miles (65 sq km)

Capital territory area: 350 square miles (906 sq km)

Altitude: 1,500–2,000 feet (457–610 m) above sea level

Average temperature: 50°F (10°C) in January; 90°F (32°C) in July

Average rainfall: 36 inches (91.4 cm) a year

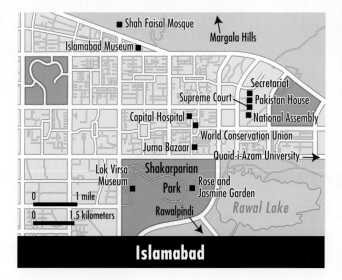

CHAPTER

Pakistanis at Work

PAKISTAN IS A VERY POOR COUNTRY. ABOUT ONE-THIRD OF all Pakistanis live below the poverty level. For the poor, good health care and education are only distant dreams. Pakistan's large population is growing, too, and refugees have added to the crunch. These are serious concerns for a government that must also support a large military force.

Almost half of Pakistan's labor force works in agriculture. Many better-educated people leave the country to find jobs. Still, Pakistan has bounced back from terrible hardships in the past. As the country becomes more stable, it can look forward to steady progress in the future.

Opposite: **A farm couple harvests wheat.**

Farming and Herding

Farming is a hard life, and droughts often make it even harder for farmers to earn a living. Farms that depend on rainfall instead of irrigation have the hardest time during droughts. Pakistan has the largest canal irrigation system in the world. About three-fourths of the farmland is irrigated by canals from the Indus River system.

Wheat, rice, and sugarcane are Pakistan's leading crops. Wheat covers more farmland than any other field crop, but in terms of value, cotton

Rice paddies in the Indus Valley

Traditional Irrigation

Digging canals from rivers is the usual way to irrigate fields. But Pakistanis also use many ancient irrigation methods. One is the Persian wheel (right). It is one of the world's oldest water-lifting devices. Buffaloes are yoked to a wooden wheel above an underground water source. Another wheel, with water pots tied around the edges, reaches down into the water. As the buffaloes trudge around and around, the pots haul water up to the surface.

Karez is an irrigation method common in Baluchistan. It uses melted snow that gathers between the rocks at the foot of a mountain. The people build an underground tunnel from the foothills all the way to their village. These tunnels can be many miles long. From the village, the water can be channeled out to the fields.

Tube wells are popular in the Punjab. They are made by driving a metal tube deep into the ground until it reaches water. Then an electric or diesel engine pumps the water up to the surface. The water irrigates fields and is drunk by cattle.

brings in the most income. It is processed into thread, yarn, and cloth. Maize (corn) is another important crop.

More than half of Pakistan's land area is used for grazing animals. Much of this land is rocky, rough, and dry. Many people in the mountain areas are nomadic herders. As the seasons change, they move their herds to better grazing grounds. They raise long-haired, shaggy mountain goats and sheep. Herders in Baluchistan raise camels.

A nomadic herder tends his flock.

Cattle help farmers with daily chores and provide milk for consumption.

A family sorts through its apricot harvest, placing the fruit on mats for drying.

Many farmers keep water buffaloes and dairy cattle. The massive buffaloes are good for pulling plows and carts. Buffalo milk is an important food, too. People drink it fresh or make it into yogurt, butter, and cheese.

Pakistan's fruit-tree orchards yield apricots, mangoes, mandarin oranges, grapefruit, apples, and dates. In some villages, the rooftops are covered with apricots drying in the sun. Farmers in the Punjab and Sind raise many varieties of mangoes, called the king of fruits. Quetta, in the west, is known as the fruit garden of Pakistan. Farmers there grow plums, peaches,

pomegranates, and apples, as well as pistachios and almonds. Spicy herbs such as coriander and cumin are other Pakistani farm products.

Manufacturing

Pakistan's manufacturing industry is small, but it is growing. Textile mills make cloth from cotton, silk, and jute. Jute is a tough, glossy plant fiber used to make sacks and twine. Pakistan makes much of its cloth into clothes. Factories also produce leather goods such as shoes, boots, and coats.

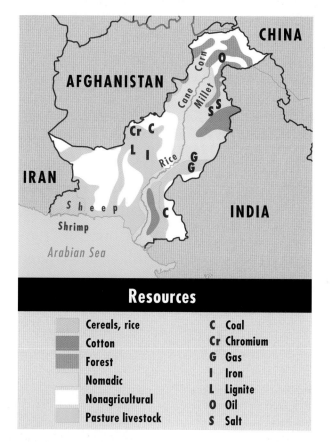

Resources

▨ Cereals, rice	C Coal
▨ Cotton	Cr Chromium
▨ Forest	G Gas
Nomadic	I Iron
☐ Nonagricultural	L Lignite
▨ Pasture livestock	O Oil
	S Salt

Textile production is one of the most important industrial sectors in Pakistan, accounting for more than half of the country's exports.

Foods are important products, too. Pakistan processes wheat into flour and sugarcane into sugar. Milk is turned into powdered milk, yogurt, cheese, and butter. Many factories make cooking oils such as vegetable ghee, similar to vegetable oil. Beverages are another important food product. Pakistan's factories also turn out petroleum products, cars, cement, fertilizer, and cigarettes.

Pakistanis produce many handcrafted goods, too, in small workshops and at home. They make beautiful, handwoven rugs and carpets. Embroidery, leather goods, pottery, and furniture are some other local handicrafts.

Handwoven baskets are a handicraft common in Pakistan.

What Pakistan Grows, Makes, and Mines

Agriculture (1999 est.)

Wheat	17,858,000 metric tons
Rice	7,733,000 metric tons
Cotton	1,912,000 metric tons

Manufacturing (June 1999–June 2000 est.)

Cotton cloth	437.4 million square meters
Refined sugar	2,429,400 metric tons
Petroleum products	50,700,000 barrels

Mining (2000 est.)

Crude petroleum	20,450,000 barrels
Natural gas	24,222 million cubic meters
Limestone	9,884,000 metric tons

Money Facts

Pakistan's basic unit of money is the Pakistani rupee. It's made up of 100 paisa. Banknotes come in values of 5, 10, 50, 100, 500, and 1,000 rupees. Coins have values of 1, 5, 10, 25, and 50 paisa and 1 and 2 rupees. (Pakistanis do not commonly use the 1-, 5-, and 10- paisa coins.) In mid-2003, U.S.$1 was equal to 57.79 Pakistani rupees, and 1 Pakistani rupee was equal to 1.7 U.S. cents.

All of Pakistan's banknotes show a picture of Muhammad Ali Jinnah, Pakistan's founding father, on the front side. Various monuments appear on the back. The 1,000-rupee note, for example, shows Jahangir's Tomb in Lahore. The Gate of Lahore Fort appears on the 50-rupee note. The 10-rupee note shows a scene of Mohenjo Daro.

A coal mine in Pakistan

Mining and Energy Sources

Pakistan's wells, mines, and quarries yield petroleum (oil), natural gas, limestone, coal, rock salt, gypsum, and silica sand. Some of the oil is refined to make gasoline, kerosene, jet fuel, and other petroleum products.

Pakistan's own oil and natural gas take care of much of its energy needs. However, the country still has to import oil from other nations. Pakistan has large natural-gas reserves, though. The government wants natural gas to be the fuel of choice in the future. It would be used as fuel to run electric-power plants.

Hydroelectric power, or water-generated electricity, is an important energy source. It is created by dams on Pakistan's rivers. "Power theft" is a problem in some areas. This happens when people illegally hook up to electric-power lines or tamper with electric meters. Nuclear power is another source of energy. In 2000 Pakistan opened its second nuclear-power plant.

Much of Pakistan's rural population has no electricity. In the mountain areas it is too hard to build power plants and hydroelectric dams. Instead, villagers build fires for cooking and warmth. For fuel they use wood, dried dung, or the leftovers from crushed sugarcane. The government is planning to develop solar power to bring electricity to rural villages. This will cut down on the villagers' need for firewood, thus conserving wood. It may also help keep people from leaving their villages for the overcrowded cities.

Tarbela Dam, along the Indus River, generates almost half of the country's hydroelectric power, making it an important energy source in Pakistan.

Weights and Measures

The metric system is Pakistan's official standard for weights and measures. But Pakistanis commonly use two other systems, too. One is the British imperial system. It uses units such as quarts, inches, and ounces instead of the metric liters, meters, and grams.

Pakistan's other system is a traditional weight system used in South Asia. Its smallest unit is the *tola*, which weighs 11.66 grams (0.4 ounce). Eighty tola equal 1 *seer* (0.933 kg/2.06 lbs.), and 40 seer equal 1 *maund* (37.32 kg/82.28 lbs.).

Since 1980, Pakistan has rounded these weights up to their nearest metric units. The seer is now considered equal to 1 kilogram (2.2 lbs.), and the maund is 40 kilograms (88.2 lbs.).

Getting Around

Mountains, rivers, deserts, and rocky terrain make it hard to get around in Pakistan. In rural areas people use donkeys or bull carts to get their products to market. Rural roads also get tractor, bicycle, and motorcycle traffic. Drivers often have to swerve or slow down for goats or cattle on the narrow roads.

People in Pakistani cities use a variety of transportation methods.

Vans, pickup trucks, jeeps, and rickety buses brave the mountain routes. In the cities, people ride buses, taxis, rickshaws, and *tongas*, or two-wheeled horse carts.

The Grand Trunk Road is Pakistan's most famous highway. It runs between India and Afghanistan. On its way, it passes through Lahore and Peshawar and on through the Khyber Pass. Now paved, the

road follows an ancient route that dates from the 1500s. The Karakoram Highway is another famous road. It runs through the Himalayas between China and Pakistan. At Khunjerab Pass, it reaches an altitude of more than 15,000 feet (4,572 m).

Pakistan's railways carry both passengers and cargo. The main railroad line runs all the way from Karachi in the south to Peshawar in the north. The national airline is Pakistan International Airlines (PIA). It flies within Pakistan as well as to other countries. The major port for international shipping is Karachi.

Decorated buses travel along the Karakoram Highway.

Sewage and rubbish surround a drainage creek in a residential area of Karachi.

Environmental Issues

When it comes to pollution control, Pakistan has a long way to go. Toxic chemicals pollute the rivers and streams. Smokestacks belch thick clouds into the air. Cities are hazy with smog from car and truck exhausts.

Pakistan is committed to developing its economy. However, progress has its drawbacks. Pakistan's factory wastes often end up in city and village water supplies. Karachi residents report that in the 1980s, they could swim and fish in their city's Lyari River. But today its waters are blackened with industrial and human waste.

As cities become more industrialized, their vehicles and factories pollute the air. A constant cloud of smog hangs over

Islamabad, the capital. Air pollution is especially bad in Karachi and Lahore, the two largest cities. Their pollution levels are twenty times higher than the standards set by the World Health Organization.

Rural areas have problems of their own. As trees are cut to make room for farmland, topsoil washes away. Vegetation is also lost to the growing population, including the influx of refugees. In addition, people clear trees and shrubs from the hillsides to fuel their cooking fires.

Some Pakistanis argue that it is too expensive to protect the environment. Besides, they would have to cut back on development at a time when they need to grow. In the early 1990s the government drew up a set of goals for protecting the environment. However, the government has been slow to provide enough funds to meet those goals. Meanwhile, the World Bank and other organizations are funding projects to protect wildlife, restore forestland, and improve irrigation. These projects empower rural people to manage their own affairs. In the cities, some neighborhoods are conducting their own cleanup campaigns. Maybe in time Pakistan will find a balance between growth and conservation.

The air in Karachi is thick with smog.

People of Many Cultures

P

AKISTAN IS A LAND OF MANY ETHNIC GROUPS AND CULTURES. Over the centuries waves of newcomers migrated over the mountains from central Asia. Aryans, Persians, Greeks, Pashtuns, and Mughals all came to the region this way.

Other groups spread across the subcontinent from present-day India. Arabs sailed the Arabian Sea and moved into Sind. Under the Mughal Empire, many more people arrived from

Opposite: **Children in northern Pakistan**

Pakistan is the seventh most populated country in the world.

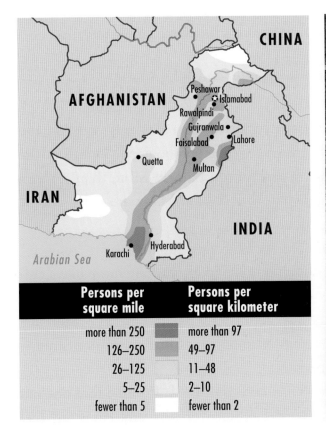

Persons per square mile		Persons per square kilometer
more than 250		more than 97
126–250		49–97
26–125		11–48
5–25		2–10
fewer than 5		fewer than 2

Population of Major Cities (1998 census)

Karachi	9,269,265
Lahore	5,063,499
Faisalabad	1,977,246
Rawalpindi	1,406,214
Multan	1,182,441
Hyderabad	1,151,274
Gujranwala	1,124,749
Peshawar	988,005
Quetta	560,307
Islamabad	524,500

the Middle East. They held positions in government and business throughout the empire. Each of these groups brought its own culture, customs, language, and point of view. Pakistan today is a blend of all these cultures.

More than 149 million people live in Pakistan, according to 2002 estimates. That gives Pakistan the seventh-largest population among the nations of the world. Most residents live along the Indus River Valley in the Punjab and Sind. The population is especially dense in the fertile irrigated region around Lahore. Baluchistan, on the other hand, is very sparsely populated. Only about two out of five Pakistanis live in cities and towns. The rest are scattered across the countryside.

Ethnic Groups and Migrations

Pakistan's major ethnic groups are Punjabi, Sindhi, Pashtun, and Baloch. More than half of all Pakistanis are Punjabi. Sindhis and Pashtuns each make up about one-eighth of the population. About 4 percent are Baloch. More than a dozen other ethnic groups live in Pakistan. Many are tribal people who dwell in the mountains.

Another group are the *muhajir*. Muhajir means "refugee." The muhajir are not an ethnic group; they are more like a cultural group. They are the Muslims who moved from India to Pakistan when the two countries separated in 1947. Muhajirs were the largest group of immigrants in Pakistan's history— about 8 million people!

Pakistan took its first census in 1951. It found that one out of four people in West Pakistan (present-day Pakistan) had

A Punjabi dance group assembles for a performance.

migrated from India. After Bangladesh broke away in 1971, thousands more Muslims moved from there to Pakistan.

In general, each ethnic group is associated with a certain region. For example, the Punjab is the homeland of Punjabis, and Sindhis are native to Sind. Balochs live in Baluchistan. Pashtuns live in the North-West Frontier Province and the Federally Administered Tribal Areas. However, there are many exceptions to this.

In Sind's larger cities, the muhajirs became the majority group. Wars in Afghanistan drove more than 3 million Afghan refugees into Pakistan. Most were ethnic Pashtuns, and they settled in refugee camps around Peshawar. But many moved into Karachi, in Sind. This added to Sind's complicated ethnic makeup.

Pakistan's Ethnic Groups	
Punjabi	58%
Sindhi	13%
Pashtun	12.5%
Muhajir (cultural group)	8%
Baloch	4%
Others	4.5%

Punjabis are the people of the former Indian state of Punjab. That state was divided when India and Pakistan were separated during partition. Thousands of Muslim Punjabis then migrated to Pakistan's side of Punjab Province. Many Punjabis today work as farmers in the Punjab's Indus Valley. Many government officials and army officers are also Punjabis.

Sindhis are mainly rural people. They are very proud of their Sindhi culture, folklore, and literature. Sindhis have often clashed with the muhajir refugees, who settled in the cities of Sind and took up jobs in business, finance, and management.

Sindhi woman

The Pashtuns work mainly as herders, farmers, and traders. Many Pashtuns are in the army, too. Pashtuns hold to a code of honor called *Pakhtunwali.* It calls for hospitality and giving shelter to any stranger, even an enemy. A *jirga*, or council of tribal elders, resolves disputes in the community.

Balochs are a nomadic people. They move their sheep and goats across the dry Baluchistan plateau. Tribal mountain people herd sheep and goats. Some also hunt wild animals for food. Others raise crops where the land is fertile.

The Kalash

The Kalash are one of Pakistan's many tribal ethnic groups. They live in the lush Chitral Valley of the Hindu Kush Mountains. Their homes are made of wood, stone, and mud, and they raise grains and goats. The Kalash, also called Kalash Kafirs, are non-Muslims who follow a religion with many gods. Dancers perform at their many colorful religious festivals.

Kalash women stand outside their wood-and-stone home.

The Kalash are light-skinned, and many even have blond hair. They are believed to be descendants of Alexander the Great's men, who once marched through the valley. Kalash women's folk costumes are similar to those in northern Greece. The Kalash of Kafiristan (in present-day Afghanistan) were the inspiration for Rudyard Kipling's story "The Man Who Would Be King."

Languages

There is no one Pakistani language. In fact, more than twenty languages are spoken in Pakistan today. Urdu is the country's main official language. Urdu originated in northern India during the Mughal period. It's related to Hindi, the major language of India. But Urdu picked up many elements of Persian and Arabic as it took shape. Urdu is written from right to left, in a Persian-Arabic script.

More than twenty languages are spoken in Pakistan.

Urdu is a first language only among the muhajir. For them, Urdu is a symbol of their Mughal culture. For most Pakistanis who speak Urdu, it's a second language. Punjabi, Sindhi, and Pashto are the most widely spoken as first languages. Other languages are Balochi, Brahui, Siraiki, Hindko, and Burushaski. English is also widely used in government and business.

Language Regions

Like Pakistan's ethnic groups, each language is linked to a specific region—but with exceptions. Punjabi is the native language of the Punjab, and close to half of all Pakistanis speak it. However, Punjabi is used in rural areas more than in the cities. It is mostly a spoken language rather than a written one. Schools in the Punjab teach in Urdu, and their students graduate knowing how to read and write Urdu. Siraiki is a blend of Punjabi and Sindhi. It is spoken in places where the two groups overlap.

Sindhi is the native language in Sind. Before 1947, most of Sind's educated people were Hindus. After 1947 millions of them moved to India. However, a large minority community of Sindhi-speaking Hindus still lives in Sind.

Sindhi speakers have struggled fiercely to preserve their language. Urdu- and Punjabi-speaking muhajirs swarmed into Sind after 1947. In many areas Sindhi speakers found themselves a minority in their own land. They felt their own language and culture were being smothered. Violent ethnic

Common Words

(Words are spelled according to pronunciation or the standard Latin-alphabet version.)

English	Urdu	Punjabi	Sindhi	Pashto
hello	assalaam-o-alaikum	sat sri akal	salam	senga yai
(response)	wa-alaikum salaam			
good-bye	alwidah	fir milange	khoda haliz	paamaha
				dekha *or* de uday pa aman
yes	jee haan	aaho *or* ha ji	ha	ho
no	nahin	nahi	na	ya
one	ek	ik	hiku	yaw
two	do	do	ba	dwa
three	tin	tin	ti	dre

riots broke out in Sind in the 1970s. Eventually, the government gave Sindhi special status. It's now taught in Sind schools along with Urdu.

Many other languages are spoken by Pakistan's tribal groups. The Pashtun people of the North-West Frontier Province speak Pashto. Balochi is the major language in Baluchistan. Many Balochs also speak Brahui. Burushaski speakers live in the mountainous Hunza and Yasin regions of Pakistan's Northern Areas. Hindko is spoken in many of the high mountain valleys of the North-West Frontier Province and northern Punjab.

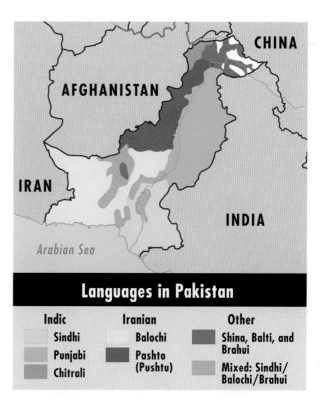

Languages in Pakistan

Indic	Iranian	Other
Sindhi	Balochi	Shina, Balti, and Brahui
Punjabi	Pashto (Pushtu)	Mixed: Sindhi/Balochi/Brahui
Chitrali		

Spiritual Life

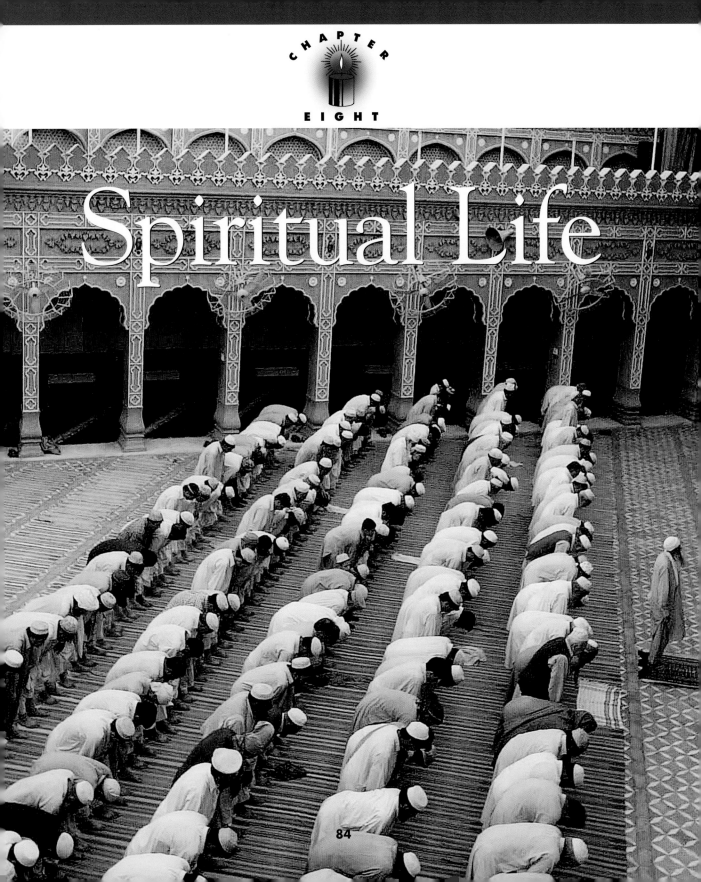

Islam is Pakistan's state religion. Indeed, the overwhelming majority of Pakistanis are Muslims. Pakistan's constitution, however, also calls for religious freedom. The largest religious minorities are Hindus and Christians. Small communities of Sikhs, Parsis (descended from Persian refugees), and Buddhists live in Pakistan, too. Non-Muslims make up only about 3 percent of the entire population.

Islam means "submission to God." Muslims are "those who submit." For Muslims, God's name is Allah. Islam's most basic belief is that there is only one God. Thus Islam is one of the world's three great monotheistic (one-god) religions, along with Christianity and Judaism.

Muslims believe that God sent many prophets to earth to guide and teach people. Those prophets began with Adam and continued through Abraham, Moses, David, Jesus, and many others. The final prophet was Muhammad. Muslims believe he completed the teachings of all earlier prophets.

The Birth of Islam

Muhammad, called the Prophet, founded Islam in the A.D. 600s. He was born in Mecca, on the Arabian Peninsula. In about 610, Muhammad began receiving revelations from God through the angel Gabriel. These revelations were written down in the Qur'an (or Koran)—Islam's holy scriptures. Muhammad gained many followers, but his teachings were

Religions of Pakistan	
Sunni Muslim	77%
Shiite Muslim	20%
Hindu, Christian, and others	3%

Muhammad, the Prophet

Muhammad was born around A.D. 570 in the city of Mecca, in present-day Saudi Arabia. Mecca was an important trade center for caravans passing through. Even then it was a pilgrimage destination, just as it is today. Pilgrims traveled there to honor local gods at a holy shrine called the Ka'abah. Muhammad's family belonged to the clan that provided food and drink to pilgrims who came to worship there.

Muhammad was orphaned as a child and was raised by his grandfather. He lived for many years among the desert nomads. There he tended sheep and camels and learned the nomadic way of life. As a young man, he joined his uncle on his travels with trade caravans. Then in 610, according to Islamic tradition, the angel Gabriel appeared to Muhammad and revealed to him the word of God. Now Muhammad began to preach Islam and its message of Allah as the one god.

Muhammad's teachings were not welcome in Mecca. The idea of one god threatened the thriving trade that depended on pilgrims. His life in danger, Muhammad fled with his followers to Medina in 622. To defend Islam, Muhammad fought many battles with Arab tribes. In 630 he returned to Mecca, where he destroyed the old images in the Ka'aba shrine and changed the site into a mosque. By the time he died in 632, in Medina, most of Arabia paid homage to Islam.

not popular with most Meccans. They drove him out in 622, and he fled to the city of Medina. This flight is called the *hijra*, or hegira. That year marks the beginning of the Islamic calendar—and of the Islamic community itself.

In Medina, Muhammad and his disciples laid the groundwork for the Islamic way of life. The Prophet's teachings, sayings, and actions were collected to make up the *hadith*. These writings became the basis of the Sunna—Islamic social and legal tradition. Islamic law was outlined in the shari'a. These sources, along with the Qur'an, still influence Muslim life today.

Muhammad's successors were called caliphs. In the years to come they extended the Muslim universe through the Middle East, North Africa, much of Asia, and even Spain.

Today Islam is the world's second-largest religion, after Christianity. More than 1 billion people around the world are Muslims. And Pakistan has one of the highest Muslim populations in the world.

The Five Pillars

Muslims practice their faith through the Five Pillars of Islam. The first is the *shahada,* or declaration of faith: "There is no god but God (Allah), and Muhammad is the messenger of God." The second is *salat*—that is, praying five times a day. The third pillar is *zakat,* or giving alms to the poor. The fourth is *sawm,* or fasting during the holy month of Ramadan. And the fifth pillar is the *hajj*—making a pilgrimage to the holy city of Mecca at least once in one's lifetime.

At the five daily prayers, Muslims kneel and bow low, facing the city of Mecca. Prayer times are dawn, noon, midafternoon, sunset, and nightfall. The prayers are verses from the Qur'an, said in Arabic. Ideally, people pray in a mosque, but they can pray anywhere. Shopkeepers interrupt their business and farmers leave their plows to pray. Many people kneel on special prayer rugs to make their devotions.

Prayers can take place anywhere. This man prays by train tracks.

Thousands of Muslims make the trip to Mecca and the Grand Mosque in Saudi Arabia every year.

Zakat consists of charitable donations to the poor. It's based on the idea that all things belong to Allah. Zakat is a way to spread one's wealth around to less fortunate members of the community. The zakat should equal 2.5 percent of a person's wealth, to be paid every year. Some banks can deduct zakat from people's bank accounts. In other cases people make the donations on their own. Zakat funds are distributed to many causes. They go to hospitals, unemployed people, and students who cannot afford school. Some funds even provide dowries, or marriage gifts, for deserving girls.

The hajj, or pilgrimage to Mecca, is not required of people who are not well or who cannot afford it. Still, thousands of Pakistanis make the trip every year. The time for the hajj is in the twelfth month of the Islamic year. The feast of Eid ul-Azha marks the end of the hajj. Muslims around the world celebrate this feast.

The Good Life

All Muslims are required to practice the Five Pillars. Many other good works and virtues, while not required, are considered part of being a good Muslim. They include generosity, cleanliness, hard work, courage, and honesty. A man is the head of his family, yet he should treat family members kindly. A wife is expected to obey and respect her husband and care for her children. Children, in turn, are asked to respect their parents. The whole community must protect and help widows, orphans, and poor people.

In prayer, Allah is often addressed as "the most compassionate, the most merciful." As Allah embodies these qualities, Muslims are urged to show compassion and mercy toward others, too. Whenever anyone asks for help, a good Muslim responds with kind assistance.

Certain acts are forbidden by the Qur'an. They include eating pork, drinking alcoholic beverages, gambling, and charging interest when lending money. Murder, stealing, and adultery are serious crimes with harsh punishments. However, the Qur'an discourages acting out of revenge for wrongdoing.

Worship and Study

Friday is the Islamic holy day. Like other Islamic holidays, it really starts at sundown the previous day. Schools and businesses close, and the faithful attend services in the mosque.

The mosque is the Islamic house of worship. From its tall minaret, or tower, the *muezzin* calls the faithful to prayer five times a day. A mosque is usually built around a courtyard with

Above left: **Mosques are Islamic houses of worship.**

Above right: **A man washes his feet before entering a mosque to pray.**

a fountain. There the faithful perform a ceremonial washing of their hands, face, and feet before going in to pray. They leave their shoes outside the door before entering.

Inside is a glorious open space, where tall pillars rise to the ceiling. Prayer rugs cover the floors. While men and boys pray in the main hall, women and girls worship in curtained galleries along the sides or the back. On the wall opposite the entrance is the *mihrab*, a niche where the prayer leader kneels. The mihrab is a holy spot. All mosques are aligned toward Mecca, so the mihrab is the mosque's closest point to the holy city. Mihrabs are often decorated with mosaic tile patterns of Qur'an verses in Arabic calligraphy, or elegant handwriting.

Built during the Mughal Empire, Badshahi Mosque is one of the largest in the world.

Many great mosques stand in Pakistan. Badshahi Mosque in Lahore and Faisal Mosque in Islamabad are among the largest in the world. Badshahi Mosque was built in 1673 under the Mughal Empire. Its huge domes and eight minarets can be seen from far away. In contrast, Faisal Mosque is a modern structure. Lahore's Wazir Khan Mosque, built in 1643, is famous for its beautiful decorations. Its colorful glazed tiles and mosaics form elaborate patterns of flowers and calligraphy.

The modern Faisal Mosque

A boy recites Qur'anic verses during class in the Wazir Khan Mosque in Lahore.

Boys and young men study in a *madrasa*, or religious school. They memorize and recite verses of the Qur'an and write them out. For many children, this is their only education. Girls cannot attend madrasas, but many of them study at home. Some Pakistani madrasas have been suspected of teaching extremist religious views that support violence. The government has closed some of these schools, hoping to cut down on terrorist activities.

Islamic Sects

There are two main sects, or branches, of Islam—Sunni and Shiite—as well as several minor sects. Each sect grew out of heated disputes in past centuries. These quarrels were about who held spiritual authority over Muslims after the Prophet's death.

Most Muslims in Pakistan belong to the Sunni sect. Sunnism is also the major branch of Islam throughout the world. Sunni Muslims believe the leadership of Islam passed on through the caliphs, or leaders, chosen by the Muslim community. Within the Sunni sect are four divisions. Each one has a different view of Islamic law. Most of Pakistan's Sunnites belong to the Hanafi school of thought.

People who follow the Shiite sect, the Shia, form the largest Muslim minority in Pakistan. These Shia believe that the Prophet's authority passed to his son-in-law, Ali, and Ali's descendants. Shiite Muslims became the majority sect in Iran and Iraq. In Pakistan about one out of five Muslims is Shiite. They, too, belong to any of several subsects.

The Ahmadiyah sect of Islam claims a small minority in Pakistan. They are also called Qadianis, after the Punjabi village of Qadian. That was the birthplace of Mirza Ghulam Ahmad, who founded the sect in 1889. Ahmadiyah Muslims do not see Muhammad as Islam's final prophet. The Pakistani government declared Ahmadis to be non-Muslims and banned the sect in 1984. Since then, Ahmadis have been targets of persecution. They continue to campaign for their rights.

Teachers, Scholars, and Holy Men

The *imam* is an Islamic scholar and teacher. As the spiritual head of the community, he leads prayers in the mosque. Among Sunni Muslims the imam is a guide and spiritual adviser. For Shiites, the imam plays a stronger role. He has the authority to interpret God's will for the faithful. A *mullah* is an

Islamic scholar who has had extensive religious training. The full community of mullahs is called the *ulama*.

Certain holy men are known for their saintly lives and spiritual powers. They are called *pirs*. Muslims show them great reverence and support them with food, money, and other gifts. A pir trains disciples and eventually passes on his spiritual leadership to one of them.

Traditionally, a pir is a Sufi—a Muslim mystic who gains knowledge of God through direct religious experience. Throughout history, Sufi poets have written beautiful religious poetry. In Pakistan, great Sufi pirs converted much of the rural population to Islam. They were seen as saints, and people built shrines around their tombs. Today the saints' shrines are the heart of religious life in the countryside. The faithful visit the shrines to pray for help and guidance.

Flags at this tomb in Hunza represent prayers offered for an honored saint named Hussaini.

The Islamic Calendar

Like other Islamic countries, Pakistan uses the hijri, or Islamic, calendar. Years are preceded by the letters A.H. They stand for *anno hegirae*, or year of the hijra. The years are dated from the time Muhammad made his flight from Mecca to Medina in A.D. 622.

The Islamic calendar is a lunar calendar—that is, it is based on cycles of the moon. (The Western, or Gregorian, calendar follows cycles of the sun.) Each month is 29 or 30 days long, and the full year lasts 354 days. As a result, by the Western calendar, Islamic holidays fall about eleven days earlier each year (twelve days earlier in leap years). For example, the first day

of A.H. 1425 is February 22, 2004; A.H. 1426 begins on February 10, 2005; and so on.

Muslim astronomers and scholars determine the beginning of a month by watching the moon. When the thin crescent moon first appears after a new moon, that's the first day of the month. The crescent moon's appearance differs from one region of the earth to another. Thus a holiday's date may differ by a day or two from one country to another. Some Muslim countries use various complex calculations to set dates. But Pakistan and Bangladesh rely on actual moon sightings with the naked eye.

Religious Holidays

Many Islamic religious holidays are also national public holidays in Pakistan. All schools and stores close, and Muslims celebrate with special prayers, rituals, and often elaborate feasts.

Pakistani girls decorate their palms and wrists with henna for the Eid ul-Azha in Karachi.

Pakistan's biggest holidays are the two great *Eids*, or festivals. Eid ul-Azha is also called Bari Eid—the Big Eid. It honors the willingness of the prophet Ibrahim (Abraham) to sacrifice his son to God. Eid ul-Azha occurs during the month of the hajj. Each family celebrates by sacrificing a calf, a goat, a sheep, or a camel. They divide the meat into three portions. One part is for the poor, one is for friends, and one is for the family.

Ramadan is the ninth month of the Islamic calendar. All month, Muslims eat and drink nothing from sunup till sundown. After sunset they may break their fast with a meal

(*iftar*). The end of Ramadan—Eid ul-Fitr—is a time for rejoicing and feasting. Eid ul-Fitr is also called the Small Eid (Chhoti Eid). Children receive sweets, new clothes, and small gifts of money then.

Ashoura is a holiday of mourning. It honors the day when Muhammad's grandson Hussein was martyred in battle in A.D. 680. Shia Muslims celebrate Ashoura with large, public processions. Devout Shiites whip themselves in memory of Hussein's suffering. Sunni Muslims observe the day in a quieter way.

Eid-e-Milad-un-Nabi celebrates the birthday of Muhammad, the Prophet. This is a day for praying and reading the Qur'an. People also recite poetry and stories that honor the Prophet.

National Religious Holidays

(All dates are subject to actual moon sightings.)

Eid ul-Azha	Feast of the Sacrifice	February 1 (in 2004)
		January 21 (in 2005)
Muharram	Islamic New Year	February 22 (in 2004)
		February 10 (in 2005)
Ashoura	Martyrdom of Hussein	March 2 (in 2004)
		February 19 (in 2005)
Eid-e-Milad-un-Nabi	Prophet's Birthday	May 2 (in 2004)
		April 21 (in 2005)
Ramadan	Beginning of Ramadan	October 15 (in 2004)
		October 4 (in 2005)
Eid ul-Fitr	End of Ramadan	November 14 (in 2004)
		November 3 (in 2005)

Arts, Culture, and Sports

IN MANY RURAL VILLAGES POTTERS CAN BE SEEN AT THEIR wheels. They begin with a lump of wet clay and skillfully form it into a shape with their hands as it spins around on the wheel. After firing the pottery in a very hot oven, they paint it with colorful designs. Some pottery is coated with a glaze before firing. The glaze gives it a shiny finish and can make it waterproof. The Multan region is famous for its blue-glazed pottery. This style dates from the 1200s.

Opposite: **Pottery stands outside a Pakistani workshop.**

A Sindhi potter forms a wet mound of clay using a traditional potter's wheel.

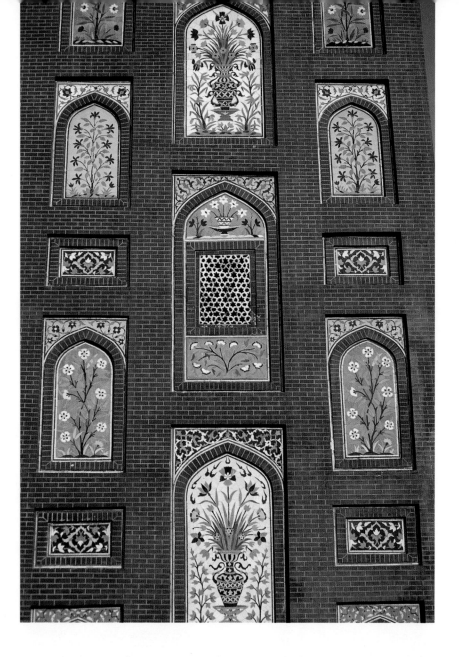

Ceramic tiles adorn the Wazir Khan Mosque.

Artisans make ceramic tiles in a similar way. They glaze, fire, and paint the tiles with geometric designs or flower-and-vine patterns. These patterns are typical of Islamic art. Depicting human or animal figures is discouraged, as it is considered a form of idolatry.

Lahore is famous for its handwoven rugs and carpets. The weavers of Lahore have made cloth and carpets since ancient times. Today the city has many modern textile mills. However, people still weave cloth on their hand looms. They may print designs on the finished fabric with wooden blocks or embroider them with beautiful needlework patterns.

Expert weavers in many other Pakistani towns make carpets, blankets, and shawls of silk, cotton, and wool. Some embroider their cloth with gold or silver thread.

Pakistani woodworkers carve furniture, trays, and room-dividing screens with intricate designs. Metalworkers make jewelry, ornaments, teapots, and tableware out of silver, brass, copper, and gold. Other craft workers make glass, marble, and camel skin into finely crafted—and useful—works of art.

An Afghan refugee weaves a carpet in a Pakistani factory.

Classical Arts and Architecture

Arts and architecture blossomed during the Mughal period. Mughal emperors took great care and pride in building grand forts, palaces, mosques, and tombs. Typically, these buildings have wide-open spaces that are flooded with sunlight. This symbolizes humans' open relationship with a loving God.

Mughal architects created buildings with domes, tall pillars and towers, and arched windows and doorways. They often used white marble that glistened in the sunlight. Floors, walls, and ceilings were decorated with multicolored ceramic tiles and sometimes even inlaid with precious jewels. Pakistan's finest Mughal structures include Badshahi Mosque, Lahore Fort, and the Shalimar Gardens in Lahore. Others are the Shah Jahan Mosque in Thatta and the poet Shah Abdul Latif Bhitai's tomb near Hyderabad.

Mughal architecture can be viewed at the Shalimar Gardens in Lahore.

Both old and modern buildings are decorated with calligraphy, or artistic handwriting. The writings are verses from the Qur'an written in Arabic script. Thus the calligraphy is both a decorative art and a spiritual teaching device. (Stained-glass windows in Western churches serve the same purposes.) Calligraphy is still a popular art form today.

Bands of Arabic script decorate a mausoleum wall.

The artist Sadequain (1930–1987) is one of Pakistan's best-known modern artists. He rendered calligraphy on marble slabs, as well as paintings on canvas. Sadequain's works are on display at Galerie Sadequain in Islamabad.

National Museum of Pakistan

The National Museum of Pakistan in Karachi contains many archaeological treasures from the Indus Valley Civilization (left). It also houses ancient Buddhist sculptures from the Gandhara region. Passing from one gallery to another, a visitor sees examples of Islamic art, including miniature paintings, and ancient coins. One area protects documents on Pakistan's political history. There is also an ethnographic gallery, depicting the cultures of Pakistan's ethnic groups.

Poetry

Poetry is very popular in Pakistan, and many Pakistanis memorize long poems to recite for their friends and family. People attend *mushairas*, or poetry readings, just as they might attend music concerts. Typical poetry themes are beauty, romantic love, and the soul's love for God. The most popular form of poetry is the *ghazal*. It's a short, graceful poem usually on a love theme.

Some poets are beloved as national heroes. Pakistan's official national poet is Allama Muhammad Iqbal. He was a poet, philosopher, and political leader in the early decades of the twentieth century. Another beloved poet is Mirza Ghalib (1797–1869). He is known for writing beautiful ghazals as well as moral tales. Both Iqbal and Ghalib wrote in the Urdu and Persian languages.

Faiz Ahmed Faiz (1911–1984) is a popular modern poet who wrote ghazals in Urdu. Faiz's poetry is political. It tells of the hardships and struggles of Pakistan's lower classes. Under some of Pakistan's military regimes, Faiz was imprisoned, and his poetry was banned.

Allama Muhammad Iqbal

The poet and philosopher Sir Muhammad Iqbal (1877–1938) is Pakistan's national poet. Pakistanis gave him the honorary name Allama, meaning "the Wise."

Iqbal was born in Sialkot, Punjab. Although he was a lawyer, he became famous for his Urdu and Persian poetry in the classical style. Today his poetry is widely quoted and recited publicly.

Iqbal urged his fellow Muslims to form a separate Muslim state. Some of his most famous poems express Muslims' sadness over their lack of power. Others urge brotherhood and justice. In 1922 the British government bestowed upon Iqbal the honor of knighthood. Pakistanis celebrate his birthday, November 9, as a national holiday. The Allama Iqbal Museum in Lahore is devoted to Iqbal's life and work.

Each region and language group has its favorite poets. For Sindhi speakers, the most beloved poet is the Sufi mystic Shah Abdul Latif Bhitai (1689–1752). The Sindhi village of Bitshah, where he died, holds a three-day festival in his honor every year. Another Sufi, Bhulle Shah (1680–1753), is the best-known Punjabi poet. His spiritual poetry often questioned the religious beliefs of his time. Among Pashto speakers, the most famous poet is Khushal Khan Khattak (1613–1689). A tribal chief, he urged his people to fight against the Mughal emperors. Besides political poems, he wrote about the beauties of women and the natural world.

Folk Traditions

Each region has its traditional folktales, too. They tell of local myths, legends, and popular historical figures. Storytellers recite the tales, usually in poetry form. The story of the ill-fated lovers Hir and Ranjha is a popular folktale in the Punjab. The story is hundreds of years old, but villagers still enjoy hearing it in the village meeting place.

In many rural areas, folk theaters entertain villagers with plays based on popular myths and legends. *Naqqals* are traditional folk plays of the Punjab. They poke fun at local situations and events.

Many of Pakistan's folk traditions are preserved by the National Institute of Folk and Traditional Heritage. The institute is usually called simply *Lok Virsa* (Folk Heritage). Lok Virsa's researchers collect folktales, legends, folk songs, and oral histories. They travel among rural villagers and gather

The Greedy Monkey

A folktale of the Indus River Valley tells of a greedy monkey. He spied some grains of wheat that had fallen into a crack between the rocks. The monkey reached in and grabbed a fistful of grain. Alas, the crack was so narrow that he could not pull his fist out without letting go of his wheat. At last he gave up, pulled his hand out, and went away hungry.

The moral of the tale is, if you are too greedy, you may end up with nothing at all!

Folk Art on Wheels

Painted trucks and buses are modern folk art in Pakistan. Owners take great pride in decorating their vehicles. They are wildly painted in vivid colors, showing everything from religious symbols and calligraphy to nature scenes. Shiny ornaments gleam everywhere, and ribbons stream from antennas.

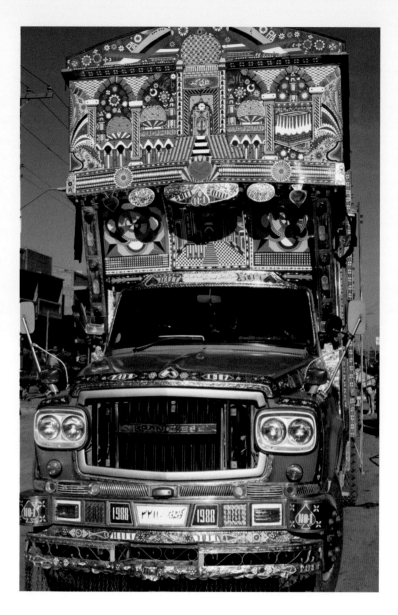

information about games, festivals, rituals, and popular sayings of the Sufi saints.

The Lok Virsa in Islamabad is a storehouse for folk-art collections. Every October, the museum holds the *Lok Mela* (Folk Festival) to show off folk artists at work.

Music, Song, and Dance

Pakistanis enjoy many styles of music. *Qawwali* is a type of devotional song. Originally, qawwali were melodic poems sung at the shrines of Sufi saints. They are still popular today, as people enjoy their beautiful melodies. The singer Nusrat Fateh Ali Khan brought qawwali to thousands of new fans with his modern style.

Ghazal poems in song form are also popular. So are traditional folk songs. Both are light and enjoyable for "easy listening." Nur Jahan is the most popular singer of Urdu and Punjabi songs today. Malika Pukraj is best known as a ghazal singer.

Pakistani folk songs cover a wide range of moods and subjects. They may herald the coming of the rains, express hope for the planting season, or rejoice in the harvest. Some tell well-known legends of couples in love. Others express the simple joys of daily life. People in rural areas enjoy their own regional Punjabi, Sindhi, and Pashto folk songs.

On radio and television, Pakistanis often hear music from popular Pakistani and Indian movies.

In both Pakistan and India, classical-music compositions are called *ragas*. A raga is built on a set of five to seven melody notes, and each raga has its special rhythmic pattern. The performer improvises on this framework. Each raga is designed for a certain mood, time of day, or state of mind.

A musician sings mystical songs at the shrine of a Sufi poet.

These men play the traditional sitar (left) and tabla.

The sitar and the tabla are the primary instruments for playing ragas. The sitar is a long-necked, guitarlike instrument made from a gourd and teakwood. It has six or seven "playing" strings and nineteen "sympathetic" strings, which are not played, but vibrate to add a fuller sound. The tabla is a pair of drums played with the fingers and the palms.

Another traditional instrument is a drum called the *dhol*. It's especially popular in rural Sind and Punjab. The dhol is played at festivals and weddings, as well as at harvest time. Many Sufi saints of the Punjab used to dance to the beat of the dhol.

Pakistani folk dances are colorful and joyful. In the Punjab men dance the *bhangra* at festivals, fairs, and weddings. Another men's dance is the *jhoomer*. It is performed in a circle while spinning around. Punjabi women in brightly colored clothing dance the *giddha* to celebrate a wedding or the birth of a child. A tribal people called the Bazigars are known for their acrobatic performances. They earn their living by performing at festive events.

Pakistani classical dance grew out of Indian classical dance. That presents a problem in Muslim Pakistan, as Indian dance is deeply rooted in Hindu traditions. Classical dances are sensuous, too, and can conflict with the Muslim sense of decency. To give a public performance, a classical dancer must first get a permit from the government's cultural office. The manager of the performance space must see that permit before the show.

Kalash women dance a traditional folk dance.

Traditionally, parents arrange their children's marriages. Love and romance have no place in this system. The bride and the groom may not even have met each other before their wedding day. "It's a system that works," says one Pakistani. "We fall in love after marriage." Nevertheless, there has been some change in this pattern in recent years.

In rural areas girls marry as early as age thirteen or fourteen, but boys are usually older. A young man's relatives spend a long time deciding on a suitable girl for him to marry. They consider her family's heritage, reputation, social status, and wealth. After they make a decision, they visit the girl's house to offer the marriage proposal to her parents. If it's accepted, the bride's family holds a *mangni*, or engagement ceremony. Once a marriage date is set, the groom and his relatives visit the girl's house again to work out details of the *nikahnama*, or marriage contract. That includes setting the *haq mehr*.

The haq mehr is a sort of protective deposit from the groom's family, as prescribed by Islamic law. It's a payment promised to the bride's family in case of divorce, abandonment, or the husband's death. It might consist of money, land, or even irrigation rights. Some brides' families set a low haq mehr of 32 rupees as a courtesy. Some families, however, demand much larger amounts. The woman's monthly maintenance allowance is also set. This is the money she needs to run her household.

All these details are drawn up in the nikahnama at the local marriage registry. After gifts are exchanged, the marriage

The Wedding

As the wedding day approaches, white lights are strung all around the bride's house. They sparkle from trees, bushes, and lampposts, as well as from the house itself. Before the wedding, female friends and relatives paint decorative patterns on the bride's hands and feet with henna paste, a reddish dye. Her hair is styled, and she puts on beautiful jewelry, clothing, and makeup.

In a traditional wedding the ceremony is held outdoors under a huge tent. The bride and the groom say special prayers and perform wedding rituals. The *quazi*, or religious leader, recites the marriage contract, and the couple sign it. Then the guests eat, sing, and dance for hours. The day

after the wedding, the groom's family invites all the guests over for a festive dinner.

agreement is settled. Then elaborate festivities make the marriage truly complete.

The bride is also given a dowry, or marriage gift, from her family. It may consist of jewelry, fine clothing, furniture, and household goods. The dowry sets the bride up for married life and remains her property after the marriage.

It can be hard for a new wife to adjust to married life. She enters her husband's household and must get used to his family's habits, customs, and rules. Her mother-in-law may insist on her own methods of cooking, cleaning, and child care. The bride may also have to work out friendly relations with her sisters-in-law.

Arts, Culture, and Sports **111**

Primary school is provided free of charge to all school-age children.

Education

Pakistan's population is growing so fast, it's hard for the government to open enough schools for all the students. The constitution guarantees free public education for all primary-school-age children. Primary school usually begins at age five and lasts five years. School attendance is not required. In 1996 about 74 percent of primary-school-age children in Pakistan actually attended school. The majority of these students were boys. Fewer than half of the girls in that age group attended school. Now the government is working to give a basic education to all children. Wealthy families can afford to send their children to good private schools.

Secondary school begins at age ten. It lasts seven years—a three-year stage, followed by a four-year stage. Attendance in secondary schools is much lower than in primary schools. Many older children quit school to help their families.

Peshawar University

Fewer than half of adult Pakistanis can read and write.

Pakistan has more than twenty public colleges and universities. They include Quaid-i-Azam University in Islamabad and the universities of Karachi, Peshawar, and Sind. Three private universities teach specialized subjects. They are Lahore University of Management Sciences, Aga Khan Medical College in Karachi, and Ghulam Ishaq Khan Institute of Engineering Sciences and Technology in the North-West Frontier Province. There are also many trade schools that teach agricultural techniques.

Pakistan has one of the world's lowest rates of literacy—that is, the ability to read and write. In 2000 only about 43 percent of Pakistani adults could read and write. Here, too, the percentage of men surpassed that of the women.

Arts, Culture, and Sports   **113**

Cricket—a type of ball-and-bat game—is Pakistan's national sport. Every major town has its own local teams, and players on the national team are nationwide heroes. A cricket match lasts all day, so fans have a whole day to keep up the excitement. Nothing has topped the excitement of the 1992 season, when Pakistan beat England to win the cricket World Cup. The 1999 season was a big one, too. Pakistan reached the finals, only to lose to Australia.

Squash, soccer, and field hockey are also popular sports. Like cricket, these were introduced during British colonial times. Squash is a cross between handball and tennis. Players use a racket to hit a ball against a wall, hoping their opponent cannot return it. Some of the world's greatest squash players have been Pakistanis.

Pakistani batsman Salim Elahi plays a sweep shot against England at their 2000 cricket match at Iqbal Stadium in Faisalabad.

Squash Power

Two Pakistani squash champions have reigned as the number-one players in the world. Jehangir Khan (1963–) is known as the most successful player in the history of squash. In 1981, at the age of seventeen, he won both the British squash championship and the World Open championship. By the time he retired in 1993, he had won the World Open six times and the British Open ten times. Jehangir is now the manager of Pakistan's Squash Committee.

Jansher Khan (1969–) is another powerhouse player. (He is not related to Jehangir Khan.) By 1997 he had won eight World Open squash titles and six British Open titles. He retired from the game in 1999 but announced a comeback in 2002.

Kabaddi is a team sport that is also played in India, Australia, and many Asian countries. It's a type of tag game that requires considerable lung power. Two teams face each other across the playing field. The "raider" from one team takes a deep breath and runs toward the other team, chanting "kabaddi" over and over. He tags, or touches, as many opposing players as he can and then returns to his team's side before that one breath runs out! Continuing his chant proves that he's not taking another breath. His team gets a point for every opposing player he tags.

The game of polo arrived in Pakistan from central Asia in the 1200s. This horseback sport began as a training game for soldiers. Every year, a famous polo tournament is held in the Shandur Pass, high in Pakistan's northern mountains. It is an exciting match between the traditional rival teams of Gilgit and Chitral.

In ancient times, Pakistanis and Indians learned wrestling for combat and self-defense. Today their unique form of

A traditional wrestling match in Sind

wrestling is a national sport in both countries. Wrestlers grapple in an earth-filled pit (*akhara*) measuring about 20 feet (6 m) on each side. Competitions (*dungals*) are held throughout Pakistan. Champion wrestlers (*phelwans*) win the Gurz, a gold or silver trophy inlaid with precious stones. The Pakistani city of Gujranwala is known as the City of Wrestlers because so many champions have come from there.

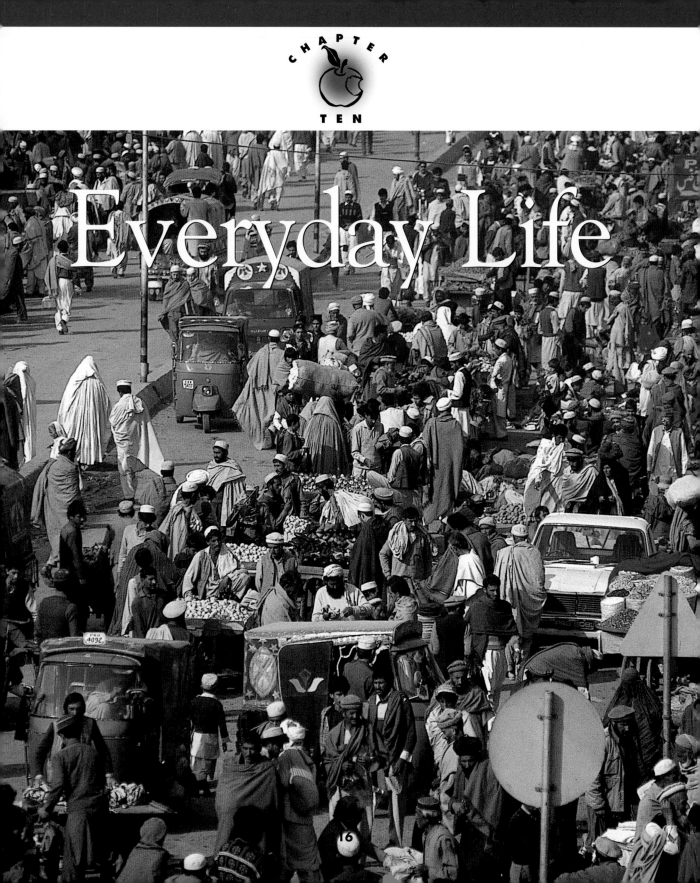

Everyday Life

Downtown areas in Pakistani cities are crowded and hectic. Traffic seems to move without rules, as drivers speed and switch lanes to get ahead. Cars, trucks, and buses compete with bikes, motorcycles, donkey carts, and chickens. Three or four people manage to pile on one bike, and passengers cling to the sides of overpacked buses. Now and then a water buffalo waddles down the road.

Along the streets, merchants sell their goods from shops, stalls, and carts. Narrow lanes in the cities' old sections are

Opposite: **A crowded street in downtown Peshawar**

A merchant sells fresh vegetables from his stall in Quetta.

Public Holidays

These are Pakistan's nonreligious national holidays.

Pakistan Day	March 23
Labor Day	May 1
Pakistan Independence Day	August 14
Defense of Pakistan Day	September 6
Allama Iqbal Day	November 9
Birthday of Quaid-e-Azam	December 25

crowded with people buying, selling, cooking, and eating. Many cities have a weekly market day, too. Then people from the villages bring in their fresh farm products and handcrafts to sell.

Pakistan's biggest cities seem to be bursting at the seams. Every year thousands more people leave their rural villages and pack into the cities, hoping to find work or at least a better life. Cities do not have adequate housing for all these people. Some live in cramped houses in teeming neighborhoods. Others live in makeshift shacks of cardboard or sheet metal. They have no electricity or running water, and diseases spread easily.

Middle-class and wealthy people are much more comfortable. They live in large apartment buildings or in single-family homes in good neighborhoods. They enjoy modern conveniences such as televisions, videocassette recorders, and computers. They have a better education, are familiar with other cultures, and often speak English as a second language. Many well-to-do families have servants and can afford to send their children to private schools.

Stacks of hay are stored on the roof of this stone farmhouse.

Village Life

In rural villages, life moves much more slowly and quietly. Cars, trucks, and motorcycles may sometimes zoom down the dirt roads, raising clouds of dust. But most people travel on foot or by donkey or cart.

Many villages are built in a circle so that their homes' back walls create a sort of barrier to the outside. In the center of town are the mosque, the school, the village well, and a market space. Roads run out from the center to homes and fields. In the mountains, villages may be built on the hillsides with each house facing outward.

Villagers build their homes of sun-dried mud, clay, or bricks. These materials are great for keeping the homes cool in the summer and warm in the winter. A walled courtyard in front of the home provides a social area, a place for sleeping during hot weather, and a pen for animals. Cattle often roam freely around the buildings.

Rural houses usually have two or three rooms with little or no furniture. Mats cover the earthen floors. People sleep on the mats and sit there to eat and socialize. Women cook on small kerosene or wood stoves. They may wash clothes on a riverbank, chop wood for the fire, and carry water from a river or a well to the house. Boys help their father with the farm labor, while girls share their mother's household chores.

Many rural areas have no electricity. People in electrified areas usually have at least a radio. If they can afford it, they get television sets to watch cable shows and videocassette recorders to watch movies.

In rural Pakistan a Sindhi woman prepares a meal over an open flame.

Clap Clap, Snap Snap

"Clap Clap, Snap Snap" is a popular children's game in Pakistani schools. Four to eight children stand in a circle. To begin, one person calls out a topic or a category. It should be a topic that lends itself to lists, such as birds or countries. Then everyone begins to clap his or her hands twice and snap his or her fingers twice, over and over. Each player gets two hand claps to think of something in the category and two finger snaps to call it out. Whoever cannot think of an answer quickly enough is out. Each topic lasts two rounds before a new topic is called.

Family Relations

Family ties in Pakistan are much stronger than ethnic, regional, or national loyalties. Family members and relatives are a person's main social group, and children often come along with their parents when they visit friends or attend events. Children rarely leave home before they get married. Pakistanis tend to have large families because children are considered gifts from God.

A family gathers for a photograph in Hunza.

The father or another older male is the head of the household. When a girl marries, she goes to live with her husband's family. Thus a typical household might consist of an older married couple, their sons, their sons' wives and children, and any unmarried daughters. When the father dies, his sons usually move out and set up their own households. Families take care of their elderly relatives. In the cities, however, people tend to have smaller households.

Male kinship is an important bond in Pakistan. People are considered relatives if they are related through the male line. Altogether, the related males in an extended family make up a *biradari*. Members of a biradari often live in the same village. They help one another's families in times of need and share holidays and family celebrations.

The practice of male domination varies by region and ethnic group. Married women still keep in touch with their own families. In some places, the woman's relatives play a large role in family and community life.

Boys and Girls, Men and Women

"We don't have any relationship with boys," says a young Pakistani girl. "Girls cannot have boyfriends in our culture, as it is against the teachings of our religion."

In Pakistan dating is not a custom as it is in Western countries. Boys and girls play together when they are young. But as they grow older, they can no longer socialize freely. Boys and girls attend separate schools and worship in different sections of the mosque. Ordinarily, teenage girls can go out of the house only if they have a chaperone.

Women and older girls may not have social or physical contact with men outside their families. Even a married couple should not hold hands or hug in public. Men and women are seated separately in restaurants, theaters, and mosques. In the most traditional families, the women are in *purdah*—that is, they are totally shielded from public view. Many homes have a guest space for receiving visitors, while the women stay out of sight in other rooms.

Not all families hold to such strict traditions. Many women in Pakistan are well educated. They may work as doctors, teachers, engineers, or government officials. If they stay home to care for their families, it is their own choice. The vast majority, however, have no choice. Their role in life has been decided by their families and the standards in their communities. Little by little, women in Pakistan are beginning to realize that they have choices, abilities, and rights.

Clothing

Pakistan's national dress style is simple and comfortable for the climate. Clothing is also designed to be modest according to Islamic law. Both men and women wear the *shalwar qamiz*. This consists of baggy pants and a long, loose shirt with side splits. Another popular style is flared trousers called *sherwani* with an A-line shirt, the *kurta*.

These men wear Pakistan's tradtional baggy pants and long, loose shirts.

Long, colorful headscarves, or dupattas, are worn by Pakistani women.

Men's clothing usually comes in solid, plain colors. For formal occasions, they may wear a colorful vest or coat. In the cities, however, some men wear Western clothing—a suit or a shirt and slacks. Men may wear a turban or a cap on their heads. Each region has its own style of turban.

Women's clothing is much more colorful than men's. Women also wear a *dupatta*, or long headscarf. Some women wear a shawl called the *chador* over their head and shoulders. In public some wear the *burqa*. This garment covers the body from head to toe. Still, there are women who wear no head covering at all.

Different regions have their own variations in dress. Some Punjabi men and women wear a loose skirt instead of pants. Clothing in the Peshawar area reflects its rough, frontier lifestyle. There, men wear pistols at their sides and bandoliers of bullets across their chest. Tribal people in the mountains wear various colorful clothing styles.

Food

Pakistani food is a mixture of Indian, Persian, Arab, and Turkish foods. Most food is made from simple, fresh farm products such as wheat, vegetables, meat, and milk. Herbs, seeds, and other flavorings often spice up the dishes.

A typical meal includes rice (*chawal*), vegetables (*sabzi*), meat (*gosht*), and a flat bread (*roti*). *Naan* is the most popular bread. It is a flat, leavened bread baked in a *tandoor*, or clay oven. Round flat breads called *parathas* (often stuffed with vegetables or meat) and *chapatis* are favorites, too. Rice is usually simply boiled. Women prepare a rice dish called *biryani* for special occasions. They cook the rice with a yogurt-and-meat sauce and flavor it with saffron.

A street vendor in Karachi sells his food to passersby.

Kheer

This Pakistani rice pudding makes a light, refreshing dessert. Makes 8 to 10 servings.

$\frac{1}{2}$ cup rice

2 quarts milk

2 tablespoons cornstarch

$1\frac{1}{2}$ cups sugar

$\frac{1}{4}$ to $\frac{1}{2}$ teaspoon cardamom

$\frac{1}{4}$ to $\frac{1}{2}$ teaspoon cinnamon

$\frac{1}{4}$ to $\frac{1}{2}$ teaspoon ground cloves

Crushed almonds

Soak the rice in water for about 15 minutes, then drain it. Set aside 4 tablespoons of the milk in a bowl. Put the rest of the milk in a large saucepan, and add the rice. Cook over low heat for about 20 minutes, until it comes to a slow boil and the rice begins to get soft. Add the cornstarch to the milk that was set aside, and mix until it makes a paste. Add the paste to the boiling rice and milk. Stir until the mixture thickens. (This will not take very long.) Add the sugar, cardamom, cinnamon, and cloves, and bring the mixture to a boil. Remove from heat, spoon into bowls, and sprinkle crushed almonds on top of each serving.

Chicken, beef, lamb, and goat are popular meats. Both meat and vegetables are often prepared with a spicy curry sauce that can take all day to cook. Meat may also be grilled or served as kebabs. Special meat dishes include flavorful grilled chicken (*tikka*), meat curry (*korma*), and rice cooked with meat (*pilao*).

Nihari is a hearty breakfast dish that can fill up a person all day. It is made from chunks of beef cooked overnight in oil with spices and hot peppers. A more common breakfast consists of a flat, fried cake called *parata*, served with eggs.

Fresh fruits are often served for dessert. Another dessert is *kheer*, a delicious rice pudding flavored with cardamom, cloves, and cinnamon. *Halwa* is a chunky dessert made with eggs, dried fruits and vegetables, and nuts. *Shahi tukray* is made of fried bread cooked in milk or cream, sweetened with syrup, and topped with nuts. *Mithai* are desserts for special occasions. They're made with flour and milk or cream and cooked in a sweet syrup.

People often end their meal with *paan*. It is a mixture of tobacco paste, spices, and betel nut spread on a betel leaf. It's considered an aid to digestion.

Pakistanis drink *chai*, or strong tea, in both summer and winter. Chai is boiled with milk and flavored with cardamom, nutmeg, and sugar. *Lassi*, a sweet yogurt drink, and sugarcane juice are popular summer drinks. Alcoholic drinks are never served in public, as they are against Islamic law.

Hospitality to visitors—even strangers—is very much a part of the Islamic way of life. Following this tradition, Pakistanis show their hospitality by offering tea to guests in their homes or offices. Anyone who arrives at mealtime is invited to come in and share the meal. This is much more than a religious duty. It is the genuine goodwill and kindness of a warm-hearted, generous people.

Hospitality is an important value for Pakistanis.

Timeline

Pakistani History

The Indus Valley Civilization flourishes.	**c. 2500** B.C.
Aryans from central Asia conquer the Indus region and introduce their Vedic religion.	**c. 1500** B.C.
Cyrus the Great of Persia conquers the Indus region; it becomes part of the Achaemenid Persian Empire.	**500** B.C.
Alexander the Great conquers the Punjab.	**327** B.C.
Ashoka extends the Mauryan Empire and Buddhism to Pakistan.	**200s** B.C.
The Kushans under Kaniska conquer Pakistan, with Peshawar as their capital.	**c. A.D. 120–160**
The Gupta Empire rules northern India, with some control over the upper Indus Valley; arts and sciences flourish.	**300s–600s**
Islam is introduced in Pakistan.	**711**
Pakistan comes under the rule of the Muslim sultans of Delhi.	**1200s**
Much of Pakistan becomes part of the Mughal Empire.	**Early 1500s**

World History

2500 B.C.	Egyptians build the Pyramids and the Sphinx in Giza.
563 B.C.	The Buddha is born in India.
A.D. 313	The Roman emperor Constantine recognizes Christianity.
610	The Prophet Muhammad begins preaching a new religion called Islam.
1054	The Eastern (Orthodox) and Western (Roman) Churches break apart.
1066	William the Conqueror defeats the English in the Battle of Hastings.
1095	Pope Urban II proclaims the First Crusade.
1215	King John seals the Magna Carta.
1300s	The Renaissance begins in Italy.
1347	The Black Death sweeps through Europe.
1453	Ottoman Turks capture Constantinople, conquering the Byzantine Empire.
1492	Columbus arrives in North America.
1500s	The Reformation leads to the birth of Protestantism.
1776	The Declaration of Independence is signed.
1789	The French Revolution begins.

Pakistani History

Sikhs take control of Punjab, with Lahore as their capital.	**Early 1800s**
The British defeat the Sikhs; Pakistan becomes part of the British Empire.	1849
The All-India Muslim League is founded.	1906
Allama Muhammad Iqbal proposes the creation of a separate Muslim state.	1930
India and Pakistan become independent nations on August 14; Pakistan consists of an eastern and a western section.	1947
General Muhammad Ayub Khan becomes Pakistan's first elected president.	1960
India and Pakistan fight seventeen-day war over the disputed territory of Kashmir.	1965
East Pakistan breaks away and becomes the independent nation of Bangladesh.	1971
Pakistan wins the cricket World Cup.	1992
Pakistan conducts its first nuclear weapons tests.	1998
General Pervez Musharraf leads a military takeover of the civilian government.	1999
General Musharraf begins a campaign against terrorism after September terrorist attacks on the United States.	2001
India and Pakistan come dangerously close to war over Kashmir.	2002

World History

1865	The American Civil War ends.
1914	World War I breaks out.
1917	The Bolshevik Revolution brings communism to Russia.
1929	Worldwide economic depression begins.
1939	World War II begins, following the German invasion of Poland.
1945	World War II ends.
1957	The Vietnam War starts.
1969	Humans land on the moon.
1975	The Vietnam War ends.
1979	Soviet Union invades Afghanistan.
1983	Drought and famine in Africa.
1989	The Berlin Wall is torn down, as communism crumbles in Eastern Europe.
1991	Soviet Union breaks into separate states.
1992	Bill Clinton is elected U.S. president.
2000	George W. Bush is elected U.S. president.
2001	Terrorists attack World Trade Towers, New York, and the Pentagon, Washington, DC.

Fast Facts

Official name: Islamic Republic of Pakistan

Capital: Islamabad

Official language: Urdu. English is also widely used in official and business settings. Other languages: Punjabi, Sindhi, Siraiki, Pashto, Balochi, Hindko, Brahui, Burushaski, Chitrali, Shina, Balti

Karachi

Pakistan's flag

Karakorum Mountains

Religion:	Islam is the state religion.
Date of independence:	August 14, 1947
National anthem:	"Qaumi Tarana" ("National Anthem"). Words by Hafiz Jalandhari (1900–1982); music by Ahmed Ghulamali Chagla (1902–1953). Adopted in 1954.
Government:	Federal republic
Chief of state:	President
Head of government:	Prime minister
Area:	310,402 square miles (803,937 sq km)
Borders:	Iran to the southwest, Afghanistan to the west and north, China to the northeast, India to the east, and the Arabian Sea (part of the Indian Ocean) to the south
Highest elevation:	K2 (Mount Godwin-Austen) in Kashmir, 28,251 feet (8,611 m) above sea level
Lowest elevation:	Sea level along the coast
Average annual precipitation:	36 inches (91.4 cm) in Islamabad
Average January temperature:	50°F (10°C) in Islamabad
Average July temperature:	90°F (32°C) in Islamabad
Length of coastline:	650 miles (1,046 km)
Greatest distance, north to south:	935 miles (1,505 km)
Greatest distance, east to west:	800 miles (1,287 km)

Mohenjo Daro

National population: 149,277,300 (October 2002 est.)

Population of major cities (1998 census):

Karachi	9,269,265
Lahore	5,063,499
Faisalabad	1,977,246
Rawalpindi	1,406,214

Famous landmarks:

- ▶ *Badshahi Mosque,* Lahore
- ▶ *Balahisaar Fort,* Peshawar
- ▶ *Harappa,* Punjab
- ▶ *Khyber Pass,* near Peshawar
- ▶ *Kot Diji,* Sind
- ▶ *Mahabat Khan Mosque,* Peshawar
- ▶ *Mohenjo Daro,* Sind
- ▶ *Quaid-e-Azam Mausoleum,* Karachi
- ▶ *Rukn-e-Alam Mausoleum,* Multan
- ▶ *Shalimar Gardens,* Lahore
- ▶ *Taxila,* near Rawalpindi

Major products: Manufacturing: cotton clothing, cloth, and yarn; food products; petroleum products. Agriculture: cotton, rice, wheat, maize (corn), sugarcane, milk. Mining: petroleum, limestone, coal, rock salt, gypsum, natural gas.

Currency: The Pakistani rupee is the basic unit of currency. One rupee = 100 paisa. In July 2003, U.S.$1 = 57.79 rupees, and 1 rupee = U.S.$0.017.

System of weights and measures: The metric system is Pakistan's official system. There is also some use of the imperial system (feet, pounds, etc.) and of local weights (maunds, seers, and tolas)

Currency

Religious school

Benazir Bhutto

Literacy rate:	43.2 percent	
Common Urdu words and phrases:	*Assalaam-o-alaikum*	Hello
	Wa-alaikum salaam	(response)
	Alwidah	Good-bye
	Khuda hafeez.	God be with you.
	Inshalah.	God willing.
	Aap ka haal kya hal heyh?	How are you?
	Theekh heyh or *Theek thak.*	I am fine.
	Aap ka naam kya hai?	What's your name?
	Mere naam ____ hai.	My name is ____.
	Jee haan	Yes
	Nahin	No

Famous Pakistanis:	Babur	(1483–1530)
	First Mughal emperor	
	Benazir Bhutto	(1953–)
	Prime minister, 1988–1990, 1993–1996	
	Mahmud of Ghazna	(971–1030)
	Afghan sultan and ruler of the Punjab	
	Allama Muhammad Iqbal	(1877–1938)
	National poet of Pakistan	
	Muhammad Ali Jinnah	(1876–1948)
	Founder and first governor-general of Pakistan	
	Jansher Khan	(1969–)
	World champion squash player	
	Jehangir Khan	(1963–)
	World champion squash player	
	Pervez Musharraf	(1943–)
	Pakistan's head of state, 1999–	
	Ranjit Singh	(1780–1839)
	Sikh ruler of the Punjab	

To Find Out More

Nonfiction

▶ Bouchard, Elizabeth. *Benazir Bhutto: Prime Minister*. Woodbridge, CT: Blackbirch Press, 1992.

▶ Caldwell, John C. *Pakistan* (Major World Nations). New York: Chelsea House, 2000.

▶ Grolier Educational. *Fiesta! Pakistan*. Danbury, CT: Grolier Educational, 1999.

▶ Khan, Eaniqa, and Rob Unwin (contributor). *Pakistan* (Country Insights). Austin, TX: Raintree/ Steck-Vaughn, 1998.

▶ Knight, Khandijah. *Islamic Festivals* (Celebrate). Crystal Lake, IL: Heineman Library, 1997.

▶ Kuklin, Susan. *Iqbal Masih and the Crusaders Against Child Slavery*. New York: Henry Holt, 1998.

▶ Ramulshah, Mano. *Pakistan*. New York: Viking, 1992.

▶ Sheehan, Sean. *Pakistan* (Cultures of the World). Tarrytown, NY: Benchmark Books, 1996.

▶ Suhail, Zaheer Lari. *A History of Sindh*. New York: Oxford University Press USA, 1997.

▶ Swan, Erin Pembrey. *India* (Enchantment of the World, Second Series). Danbury, CT: Children's Press, 2002.

▶ Teta, Jon A. *Pakistan in Pictures* (Visual Geography). Minneapolis: Lerner Publications, 1996.

▶ Wagner, Heather Lehr. *India and Pakistan* (People at Odds). New York: Chelsea House, 2002.

▶ Yusufali, Jabeen. *Pakistan: An Islamic Treasure*. Minneapolis: Dillon Press, 1990.

Fiction

▶ Crouch, Marcus. *The Ivory City and Other Stories from India and Pakistan.* London: Pelham Books, 1980.

▶ Kipling, Rudyard. *The Man Who Would Be King.* Cutchogue, NY: Buccaneer Books, 1990.

▶ Shepard, Aaron, and Daniel San Souci (illustrator). *The Gifts of Wali Dad: A Tale of India and Pakistan.* New York: Atheneum, 1995.

▶ Siddiqui, Ashraf, Marilyn Lerch, and Jan Fairservis (illustrator). *Pakistani Folk Tales: Toontoony Pie and Other Stories.* New York: Hippocrene Books, 1998.

▶ Staples, Suzanne Fisher. *Shabanu: Daughter of the Wind.* New York: Knopf, 1989.

▶ Staples, Suzanne Fisher, and Steven Rydberg (illustrator). *Haveli.* New York: Knopf, 1993.

Videotapes

▶ *Pakistan.* 48 minutes. Lonely Planet, 1999. A guide to Pakistan's land, cities, and culture.

▶ *Children of Heaven.* 90 minutes. Majid Majidi, director, 1997. An Iranian film showing the adventures and struggles of a Muslim boy and his sister.

Web Sites

▶ **Pakistan: the Country (Getting Acquainted)**
http://www.uh.edu/~sriaz/thecountry/index.html
Includes information on Pakistan's history, culture, land, people, and government.

▶ **A Kid's Life in Pakistan**
http://library.thinkquest.org/CR0212302/pakistan.html
For a firsthand account of a Pakistani child's everyday life.

▶ **Embassy of Pakistan in Greece**
http://www.pak-embassy.gr/index.html
For basic facts about Pakistan, as well as cities, regions, culture, crafts, and events.

▶ **AskAsia: A K-12 Resource of the Asia Society**
http://www.askasia.org/
For overviews and news about Pakistan and other Asian countries; users can also make comparisons between countries.

Embassy

▶ **Embassy of the Islamic Republic of Pakistan**
2315 Massachusetts Ave. N.W.
Washington, D.C. 20008
202-939-6200

Index

Page numbers in *italics* indicate illustrations.

A

acacias (plant life), 31
Afghanistan, 49–51
agriculture, *12, 31,* 62, 63, *63,*
    65–67, 69
    fruit-tree orchards, 66–67, *66*
    Hunza Valley, 21, *21*
    Indus River and, 12
    irrigation, 22, 23, 24, 31, 63,
       64, 75
    livestock, 28, 65–66, *65*
    Persian wheel, 64, *64*
    rice, 63, *63*
Ahmad, Mirza Ghulam, 93
Ahmadiyah sect, 93
Ahmed, Qazi Hussain, *53*
air pollution, 74–75, *75*
Akbar (Mughal ruler), 42
Alexander the Great, 41
All-India Muslim League, 45, *45,* 46
Allama Iqbal Museum, 104
Alpine forests, 30, *30*
animal life, 34–37
    Asiatic black bears, 34, *34*
    Asiatic cheetah, 35
    birds, 32, *32*
    buffaloes, 66, *66*
    caracals (wildcats), 35
    flare-horned markhor (national
       animal), 36, *36*
    livestock, 28, 65–66, *65*
    makhors, 27, 36, *36*

    sand cats, 35, *35*
    Siberian ibex, 20
    snow leopards, 36–37, *37*
    straight-horned markhor, 36
    woolly flying squirrels, 34
apricots, 66, *66*
Arabian Sea, 12
architecture, 102–103, *102*
art, 39, *106*
    architecture, 102–103, *102*
    calligraphy, 103, *103*
    ceramic tiles, 100, *100*
    flower-and-vine patterns, 100
    Indus Valley Civilization, *103*
    Islamic religion and, 10
    metalworking, 101
    pottery, 98, 99, *99*
    Sadequain (artist), 103
    weaving, 101, *101*
    woodworking, 101
Aryan culture, 40
Ashoura holiday, 97
Asiatic black bears, 34, *34*
Asiatic cheetah, 35
Ayub Khan, Muhammad, 48
Azad Kashmir region, 16, 60

B

Babur (Mughal ruler), *42, 42,* 43, 133
Badshahi Mosque, 91, *91*
Baloch culture, 79, 80
Balochi language, 83

Baltistan region, 16
Baltit Castle, 21
Baluchistan Plateau, 22
Baluchistan Province, 22, 27, 60, 65,
    78, 83
Bar Valley, 20
bazaars, 26, 27
Bazigar culture, 109
bhangra (folk dance), 109
Bhitai, Shah Abdul Latif, 105
Bhutto, Benazir, 49, 58, *58,* 133, *133*
Bhutto, Zulfikar Ali, 48–49, *48,* 58
Biodiversity Action Plan, 29
biradari (male relatives), 122
birds, 32, *32*
Bitshah (village), 105
borders, 15, 17, 19
Brahui language, 83
British East India Company, 44
British imperial system, 72
Buddhism, 41–42, *42,* 85
buffaloes, 66, *66*
burqas (clothing), 124

C

calendar, 86, 95
caliphs, 86
calligraphy, 103, *103*
caracals (wildcats), 35
ceramic tiles, 100, *100*
chadors (shawls), 124
Chagla, Ahmed Ghulamali, 54

Charsada, *53*
Chaukundi Tombs, *38*
children, 8, 76, 122
Chitral Valley, 81
Cholistan Desert, 24
Christianity, 85
chukar partridge (national bird), 32, *32*
cities
    Charsada, *53*
    Faisalabad, 22, 26, 78
    Gujranwala, 78, 115
    Hyderabad, 23, 78
    Islamabad, 22, 31, *57*, 61, *61*, 78, 91
    Karachi, *11*, 23, 26, *26*, 61, 73, *74*, *75*, 78
    Lahore, 22, 26, *26*, 31, *52*, 59, 78, 91, *92*
    Mohenjo Daro, 23, 40, *40*, 69
    Multan, 22, 27, 78, 99
    Peshawar, 27, 78, 84, *116*, 124
    Quetta, 27, 78, *117*
    Rawalpindi, 22, 26–27, 61, 78
"Clap Clap, Snap Snap" game, 121
climate, 17, 24–25, 61
    flooding, 25
    monsoons, 25
climate map, *25*
clothing, 9, 123–124, *124*
coal mining, 70, *70*
coastline, 12, 17
conservation, 29, 37
constitution, 53, 54–55, 85
cricket, 114, *114*
currency (Pakistani rupee), 69, *69*
Cyrus the Great, 41

D

dams, 71
dance, *79*, 108, *109*

dating, 122
deforestation, 29
deodar cedar (national tree), 30, 31
Deosai Plains National Park, 34
deserts, 17, 24
    Cholistan Desert, 24
    Thar Desert, *24*
dhol (drum), 108
dolphins, 33
dupattas (headscarves), 124, *124*

E

East Pakistan, 47, 48
education, 8, 9, 10, 63, 92, *92*, 112–113, *112*, *113*, 118, 122
Eid ul-Azha feast, 88, 95, *95*
Eid ul-Fitr feast, 97
Eid-e Milad-un-Nabi holiday, 97
Elahi, Salim, *114*
energy, 70–71, *71*
erosion, 29
ethnic groups, 78–81
executive branch of government, 55, 56–57

F

Faisal Mosque, 91, *91*
Faisalabad, 22, 26, 78
Faiz, Faiz Ahmed, 104
families, 121–122, *121*
Federally Administered Tribal Areas (FATA), 60, 79
Five Pillars of Islam, 87–88
flare-horned markhor (national animal), 36, *36*
flooding, 25
folk dance, 109, *109*
folk songs, 107
folktales, 105–106
foods, 9, 68, 125–127, *125*

forests, 30, 31, *31*
fruit-tree orchards, 66–67, *66*

G

games, 121
Gandhara region, 41
Gate of Lahore Fort, 69
geography
    Baltistan region, 16
    Baluchistan Plateau, 22
    borders, 15, 17, 19
    coastline, 12, 17
    deserts, 17, 24, *24*
    Gilgit region, 16
    Indus Plain, 22–23
    Kashmir region, 15–16, *16*, 44, 47–48, 51
    mountain valleys, 20–21, *21*
    mountains, 12, *14*, 16, 18–21, *18*, *20*, 22
    Northern Areas, 16, 60
    size, 17
geopolitical map, *13*
Ghaffar Khan, Abdul, 46
Ghalib, Mirza, 104
Ghanta Ghar Bazaar, 26
ghazal (poetry), 104
giddha (folk dance), 109
Gilgit region, 16
Godwin-Austen, Henry, 20
golden eagles, *32*
government. *See also* provincial governments.
    common law, 59
    constitution, 53, 54–55, 85
    executive branch, 55, 56–57
    independence, 45, 47–48
    Indus civilization, 39
    judicial branch, 55, 59–60, *59*
    legislative branch, 55, 57
    Majlis-e-Shoora (parliament), 57, *57*

National Assembly, 56, 57, 60
National Security Council, 57
Pakistan People's Party (PPP), 58
prime ministers, 56, 58, 58
religion and, 56, 57, 59
Senate, 57
shari'a (Islamic law), 59–60, 80
Taliban, 50, 56
Grand Mosque, 88
Grand Trunk Road, 72–73
Great Britain, 44, 45, 53
green sea turtles, 33, 33
Gujranwala, 78, 115

H

hadith (Islamic teachings), 86
hajj (Pillar of Islam), 87, 88
handicrafts, 68, 68
haq mehr (marriage deposit), 110
Hazarganji-Chilton National Park, 27
health care, 63
henna, 111
hijri (Islamic calendar), 95
Hilton, James, 20
Himalayan mountain range, 18
Hindko language, 83
Hindu Kush mountain range, 18
Hinduism, 85
historical maps. See also maps.
    Mughal Empire, 43
    Partition of India, 47
    Silk Routes, 41
holidays
    public, 118
    religious, 95, 96–98
housing, 9, 81, 118, 119, 119
Humayan (Mughal ruler), 42
Hunza River, 20
Hunza Valley, 21, 21

Hussaini (saint), 94
Hyderabad, 23, 78
hydroelectric power, 71

I

imam (Islamic scholar), 93
independence, 45, 47–48
India, 15
Indian National Congress, 45, 46
Indus Delta, 31, 33
Indus Plain, 22–23
Indus River, 12, 15, 17, 22–23, 22,
    23, 25, 63, 71
Indus River dolphin, 33
Indus River Dolphin Reserve, 33
Indus River Valley, 15, 63, 78
Indus Valley Civilization, 10–11,
    39–40, 39, 103, 103
Iqbal, Sir Allama Muhammad,
    47, 104, 133
irrigation, 22, 23, 24, 31, 63, 64, 75
Islamabad, 22, 31, 57, 61, 61, 78, 91
Islamabad Capital Territory, 60
Islamic Democratic Alliance
    (IDL), 58
Islamic religion. See also religion.
    Ahmadiyah sect, 93
    art and, 10
    calendar, 86, 95
    caliphs, 86
    Eid ul-Azha feast, 88, 95, 95
    Eid ul-Fitr feast, 97
    Eid-e Milad-un-Nabi holiday, 97
    Five Pillars of Islam, 87–88
    foundation of, 42
    Grand Mosque, 88
    government and, 56, 57, 59
    hadith (teachings), 86
    hijri (calendar), 95

holidays, 95, 96–98
Hussaini (saint), 94
imam (scholar), 93
Ka'abah (holy shrine), 86
literature and, 10
madrasa (religious school), 92
Mecca, 87, 88, 88
mihrab (holy place), 90
mosques, 11, 11, 26, 84, 88,
    89–92, 90, 91, 92, 100, 122
Muhammad (prophet), 85–86, 97
mullahs (scholars), 93–94
pirs (holy men), 94
prayers, 87, 87, 89, 90
Qur'an (holy book), 85, 87, 89,
    92, 97, 103
Ramadan holiday, 96–97, 96
shari'a (Islamic law), 59–60, 86
Shiite sect, 92–93
Sufis (mystics), 94
Sunna (Islamic tradition), 86
Sunni sect, 92–93
ulama (mullah community), 94
"Islamization," 49

J

Jahan, Nur, 107
Jahangir (Mughal ruler), 42
Jahangir's Tomb, 69
Jalandhari, Hafiz, 54
Jamali, Zafarulla Khan, 57
Jammu region, 47–48
jasmine (national flower), 31, 31
jhoomer (folk dance), 109
Jinnah, Muhammad Ali, 45, 46, 46,
    48, 69, 69, 133
Judaism, 85
judicial branch of government,
    55, 59–60, 59

K

K2 peak, 18, 20, *20*
Ka'abah (Islamic shrine), 86
kabaddi (sport), 115
Kalash culture, 81, *81*
Kaniska (Kushan king), 41
Karachi, *11*, 23, 26, *26*, 61, 73, *74*, 75, 78
Karakoram Highway, 73, *73*
Karakoram mountain range, 18, *18*, 20
karez (irrigation method), 22, 64
Kashmir region, 15–16, *16*, 44, 47–48, 51
Keenjhar Lake, 17
Khan, Jansher, 114, 133
Khan, Jehangir, 114, 133
Khan, Jhanda, 26–27
Khan, Nusrat Fateh Ali, 107
Khattak, Khushal Khan, 105
kheer (rice pudding), 126
Khudai Khidmatgar movement, 46
Khyber Pass, 19, *19*, 27, 41
Kirthar National Park, 29
kurta (clothing), 123
Kushan dynasty, 41–42

L

Lahore, 22, 26, *26*, 31, *52*, *59*, 78, 91, *92*
Lake Haleji, 32
lakes, 17
    Keenjhar Lake, 17
    Lake Haleji, 32
    Manchar Lake, 17, 23, 32
language regions map, 83
languages, 81–83, 118
    Balochi, 83
    Brahui, 83
    Hindko, 83
    Pashto, 82, 83
    Punjabi, 82
    Sindhi, 82, 83
    Siraiki, 82
    Urdu, 9, 43, 81, 82
legislative branch of government, 55, 57
literacy rate, 113, *113*
literature, 10, 94, 104–105
livestock, 28, 65–66, *65*
local governments. *See* provincial governments.
Lok Mela (Folk Festival), 106
Lok Virsa. *See* National Institute of Folk and Traditional Heritage.
Lost Horizon (James Hilton), 20
Lower Indus Plain, 23
Lyall, Sir Charles James, 26
Lyari River, 74

M

madrasa (religious school), 92
Mahmud of Ghazna, 42, 133
Majlis-e-Shoora (parliament), 57, *57*
makhors (national animal), 27, 36, *36*
maliks (tribal elders), 60
"The Man Who Would Be King" (Rudyard Kipling), 81
Manchar Lake, 17, 23, 32
Mangklala Stupa (shrine), 26
mangni (engagement ceremony), 110
manufacturing, 67–68, *67*, *68*, 69
maps. *See also* historical maps.
    climate, 25
    geopolitical, *13*
    Islamabad, *61*
    language regions, 83
    population density, *77*
    resources, *67*
    topographical, *17*
marine life, 33, *33*
marriage, 110–111, *111*, 121, 122
Masjid-e-Tooba mosque, 26
Mecca, 87, 88, *88*
Mehgarh civilization, 39
men, 122–123
merchants, 117–118, *117*
metalworking, 101
metric system, 72
migration, 79
mihrab (holy place), 90
military, 12, 54
mining, 69, 70, *70*
Mohenjo Daro, 23, 40, *40*, 69
monsoon season, 25
Montgomerie, T. G., 20
mosques, 11, *11*, 26, 88, 89–92, *90*, *91*, *92*, 100, 122
Mount Godwin-Austen. *See* K2 peak.
mountains, 12, *14*, 16, 18–21, *18*, *20*, 22
Mughal Empire, 11, 42, *42*, 43, *43*, 45, 77–78, 81, 82, 91, 102
muhajirs (refugees), 78
Muhammad (prophet), 85–86, 97
mullahs (Islamic scholars), 93–94
Multan, 22, 27, 78, 99
mushairas (poetry readings), 104
Musharraf, Pervez, 49, 50, 54, 56, *56*, 133
music, 11, 107–108, *107*, *108*

N

Nanga Parbat peak, 18
naqqals (folk plays), 105
national anthem, 54
National Assembly, 56, 57, 60

national flag, 52, 54, *54*
National Institute of Folk and
    Traditional Heritage, 105–106
National Museum of Pakistan, 103
national parks
    Deosai Plains National Park, 34
    Hazarganji-Chilton National Park,
        27
    Kirthar National Park, 29
National Security Council, 57
natural gas, 70
natural resources map, *67*
nikahnama (marriage contract), 110
North-West Frontier Province, 19,
    27, *30*, 60, 79, 83
Northern Areas, 16, 60
nuclear power, 71

O

olive ridley turtle, 33

P

Pakhtunwali (Pashtun code of
    honor), 80
Pakistan International Airlines
    (PIA), 73
Pakistan Muslim League (PML), 58
Pakistan People's Party (PPP), 58
Pakistani rupee (currency), 69, *69*
Pashto language, 82, 83
Pashtun culture, 79, 80
Pasu Glacier, *18*
people
    Aryans, 40
    Balochs, 79, 80
    Bazigars, 109
    children, 8, 76, 122
    dating, 122
    ethnic groups, 78–81
    families, 121–122, *121*

hospitality, 127, *127*
Indus civilization, 10–11, 39–40,
    39, 103, *103*
Kalash, 81, *81*
Mehgarh civilization, 39
men, 122–123
migration, 79
Pashtuns, 79, 80
Persians, 41
population, 61, 63, 78
    Punjabi, 78, *79*, 80, 124
    refugees, 51, *51*, 78, 79
    Sindhis, 79, 80, *80*, *120*
    women, 122–123
Persians, 41
Persian wheel, 64, *64*
Peshawar, 27, 78, 84, *116*, 124
Peshawar University, *113*
petroleum industry, 70
pirs (holy men), 94
plant life, 30–31, 75
    acacias, 31
    Alpine forests, 30, *30*
    deforestation, 29
    deodars (national tree), 30, 31
    forests, 30, *30*, 31
    jasmine (national flower), 31, *31*
    poplar trees, *31*
    wildflowers, 29
poetry, 11, 31, 94, 104–105, 107
pollution, 33, 74–75, *74*
polo, 115
poplar trees, *31*
population, 61, 63, 78
population density map, *77*
pottery, 98, 99, *99*
"power theft," 71
prayers, 87, *87*, 89, 90
primary school, 112, *112*
prime ministers, 56, 58, *58*

provincial governments, 55, 60.
    See also government.
public holidays, 118
Pukraj, Malika, 107
Punjab Province, 22, 26, 60, 80
Punjabi culture, 78, 79, 80, 124
Punjabi language, 82

Q

Qadianis. *See* Ahmadiyah sect.
al-Qaeda, 50
Qasim, Muhammad bin, 42
Quaid-e-Azam mausoleum, 26
Quaid-i-Azam University, 113
"Quami Tarana" (national anthem),
    54
Quetta, 27, 78, *117*
Qur'an (Islamic holy book), 85, 87,
    89, 92, 97, 103

R

ragas (classical music), 107–108
railways, 73
Ramadan holiday, 96–97, *96*
Rawalpindi, 22, 26–27, 61, 78
reforestation, 75
refugees, 51, *51*, 78, 79
religion. *See also* Islamic religion.
    Buddhism, 41–42, *42*, 85
    Christianity, 85
    government and, 56, 57, 59
    Hinduism, 85
    Sikhism, 43, 85
    Vedic, 40
religious holidays, 95, 96–98
resources map, *67*
rice, 63, *63*
rivers
    Hunza River, 20

Indus River, 12, 15, 17, 22–23, *22*, *23*, 25, 63, *71*
Shyok River, 28
Swat River, 21
roadways, 72–73, *73*, 119
rock paintings, 39
Rohri Hills, 39
Rose and Jasmine Garden, 31
rupee (currency), 69, *69*

S

Sadequain (artist), 103
salat (Pillar of Islam), 87
sand cats, 35, *35*
sawm (Pillar of Islam), 87
sea turtles, 33, *33*
secondary school, 112
Senate, 57
September 11 attacks, 50
Shah, Bhulle, 105
shahada (Pillar of Islam), 87
shalwar qamiz (clothing), 123, *123*
shari'a (Islamic law), 59–60, 86
Sharif, Muhammad Nawaz, 49, 58, *58*
Sharif, Nawaz, 56
sherwani (clothing), 123
Shiite sect, 92–93
Shipton, Eric, 20
Shyok River, 28
Siberian ibex, 20
Sikh religion, 43, 85
Silk Route, 15, 42

Silk Routes map, *41*
Sind Province, 23, 24, 26, *26*, 33, 60
Sindhi culture, 79, 80, *80*, *120*
Sindhi language, 82, 83
Singh, Ranjit, 43, 44, *44*, 133
Siraiki language, 82
sitar (musical instrument), 108, *108*
Siwalik Hills, 39
size, 17
snow leopards, 36–37, *37*
solar power, 71
sports, 114–115, *114*
straight-horned markhor, 36
Sufi (Muslim mystic), 94
Sunna (Islamic tradition), 86
Sunni sect, 92–93
Supreme Court, 59
Swat River, 21
Swat Valley, 21
system of weights and measures, 72

T

tabla (musical instrument), 108, *108*
Taliban, 50, 56
Tarbela Dam, *71*
terrorism, 12, 50–51, *50*, 92
textile industry, 26, 67, *67*, 101
Thar Desert, 17, *24*
theater, 105
Tirich Mir peak, 18
topographical map, *17*
trade, 15, *41*, 43

transportation, 72–73, *72*, *73*, *75*, *106*, 117, 119
tribal areas, 60
tube wells, 64

U

ulama (mullah community), 94
universities, 113, *113*
Urdu language, 9, 43, 81, 82

V

Vedas (Vedic scriptures), 40
Vedic religion, 40
villages, 105, 119–120

W

water birds, 32
Wazir Khan Mosque, 91, *92*, *100*
weaving, 101, *101*
weddings, 111, *111*
weights and measures, 72
West Pakistan, 47, 48
wildflowers, 29
women, 122–123
woodworking, 101
woolly flying squirrels, 34
wrestling, 115, *115*

Z

zakat (Pillar of Islam), 87, 88
Zia-ul-Haq, Mohammad, 49, *49*

Meet the Author

ANN HEINRICHS fell in love with faraway places while reading Doctor Dolittle books as a child. Now she tries to cover as much of the earth as possible. She has traveled through most of the United States and much of Europe, as well as in the Middle East, East Asia, and Africa. Her travels in North Africa and the Middle East gave her a deep appreciation for Islamic culture and traditions, as well as a firsthand experience of Muslims' warmth and hospitality.

Ann grew up roaming the woods of Arkansas. Now she lives in Chicago. She is the author of more than one hundred books for children and young adults on American, European, Asian, and African history and culture. Several of her books have won national awards.

"To me, writing nonfiction is a bigger challenge than writing fiction," she said. "With nonfiction, you can't just dream something up—everything has to be true. Finding out facts is harder than making things up, but to me it's more rewarding. When I uncover the facts, they always turn out to be more

spectacular than fiction could ever be. And I'm always on the lookout for what kids in another country are up to, so I can report back to kids here."

Ann has also written numerous newspaper, magazine, and encyclopedia articles. As an advertising copywriter, she covered everything from plumbing hardware to Oriental rugs. She holds bachelor's and master's degrees in piano performance. But these days, her performing arts are tai chi empty-hand and sword forms. She is an award-winning martial artist and participates in regional and national tournaments.

Photo Credits